Study Commentary on Micah

A Study Commentary
on
Micah

Dale Ralph Davis

 BOOKS

EP Books
Faverdale North, Darlington, DL3 0PH, England
e-mail: sales@epbooks.org
web: www.epbooks.org

EP Books USA
P. O. Box 614, Carlisle, PA 17013, USA
e-mail: usasales@epbooks.org
web: www.epbooks.us

First published 2010

British Library Cataloguing in Publication Data available

ISBN-13 978 0 85234 717 1   ISBN 0 85234 717 0

Unless otherwise indicated, Scripture quotations are the
author's own translation.

Printed and bound in the USA by Versa Press Inc.

In memory of
JORDAN,
whom Yahweh gave — and took

Contents

Abbreviations

ABD	*Anchor Bible Dictionary*
ANET	*Ancient Near Eastern Texts,* 3rd edition.
AV	Authorized Version (King James Version)
BDB	Brown, Driver and Briggs, *Hebrew and English Lexicon*
CSB	Christian Standard Bible
DCH	*Dictionary of Classical Hebrew* (ed. D. J. A. Clines)
ESV	English Standard Version
G-K	Gesenius-Kautzsch, *Hebrew Grammar*
IDB	*Interpreter's Dictionary of the Bible*
ISBE	*International Standard Bible Encyclopedia*
JB	Jerusalem Bible
K-B	Koehler & Baumgartner, *Hebrew and Aramaic Lexicon*
NASB	New American Standard Bible (updated edition)
NBD	*New Bible Dictionary*
NBV	New Berkeley Version
NIDOTTE	*New International Dictionary of Old Testament Theology & Exegesis*
NIV	New International Version
NJB	New Jerusalem Bible
NJPS	Tanakh: A New Translation of the Holy Scriptures according to the Traditional Hebrew Text (1985)
NKJV	New King James Version
NRSV	New Revised Standard Version
REB	Revised English Bible
RSV	Revised Standard Version
TDOT	*Theological Dictionary of the Old Testament*
TEV	Today's English Version
TLOT	*Theological Lexicon of the Old Testament*

TWOT   *Theological Wordbook of the Old Testament*
ZPEB   *Zondervan Pictorial Encyclopedia of the Bible*

Introductory matters

Did Micah leave us Micah?

My father served as a United Presbyterian pastor from 1927 until his retirement in 1971. Imagine that shortly after his retirement he had written a brief synopsis of his ministry, indicating the years served and then a sketch of the locations of his congregations: about four years at Sheakleyville, Pennsylvania; nine months in Beaver, Pennsylvania; thirteen more years in his first charge in Sheakleyville, Pennsylvania; three and a half years in Newton, Kansas, in the mid-1940s; eleven years in Harrisville, Pennsylvania; and eleven years in Aliquippa, Pennsylvania. Imagine too that we had bumped into one of my father's former parishioners who remembered how deeply moved he had been by a sermon my father had preached from Ephesians 1.

How would the average Old Testament critic tend to look at data like that? First, he might say that it's very rare for any pastor to stay only nine months in a charge — that piece must be an intrusion; it looks very suspicious, after all, because he went back, allegedly, to his previous pastorate. That is very unusual, not likely. Instead, he must have simply had a long ministry (maybe eighteen years) in Sheakleyville. Second, almost all his pastorates seem to have been in western Pennsylvania. This means it's improbable that he had one in Kansas for three years or more; after all, who would move 1,200 miles from western

Pennsylvania while the Second World War was still
going on and certain wartime restrictions were in
place? Third, the last two pastorates are said to consist of eleven years each. That is suspicious. How
often would that actually happen? More likely, what
took place was that there was only *one* pastorate of
eleven years (either my father's memory was fuzzy or
some of his friends may have tinkered with his written
summary). Fourth, sadly enough, my father never
preached from the Old Testament. Well, that one
fellow had been so impressed with a sermon on Ephesians 1, and that's in the New Testament, so obviously
my father never preached from the Old! Our critic
then concludes that, contrary to the written summary,
it is likely that my father had a ministry of perhaps
thirty years, all in western Pennsylvania — contrary to
the explicit testimony he had been given.

There's a reason for this bit of foolishness. Critics
tend to deal with Micah and other prophetic books in
the same way. We have Micah's genuine prophecies in
chapters 1 – 3 — well, except for the promise of
2:12-13 (Fohrer) or half a dozen interpolations that
have also wormed their way in (Wolff). Chapters 4 – 5
obviously cannot be from Micah because they consist
of promises, and we know (from the episode in Jer.
26:18) that Micah was remembered for his message of
judgement — hence he couldn't have spoken the
positive messages in chapters 4 – 5.[1] Chapters 4 – 5
presuppose the fall of Jerusalem (4:8), the exile and
dispersion (4:6-7) and the demise of the Davidic
dynasty (5:1) — one couldn't speak of such things
unless they had already taken place (i.e., there's no
such thing as 'predictive' prophecy). For the same
reason the prophecy of 4:1-5 could not have arisen
until after the rebuilding of the temple in the post-
exilic period, 200 years after Micah's own time (Wolff).
The bits and pieces in chapters 6 and 7 come from the
400s BC from various groups of prophets; scholars

cannot be very sure how they originated — the one thing they are certain of is that they did not come from Micah. So chapters 1 – 3 contain the only genuine preaching we have from Micah — except, of course, for later additions that have crept in even there. Read a critical discussion on the book of Micah. See if it doesn't read like pages of chaotic guesswork.[2] After summarizing scholarly study of Micah, Brevard Childs concludes that 'the growing confusion over conflicting theories of composition has increasingly buried the book in academic debris'.[3] One can hardly blame folk for being turned off towards the Old Testament; scholars have done their best to make it dull, boring and complicated.

A map of Micah

Let's leave the 'How much of Micah comes from Micah?' issue for the moment and look at the book as we have it. Just take a naïve view. How is the book put together? Maybe things are not as complicated as some people think.

There seem to be three major chunks in Micah's prophecy, each of them introduced with the imperative plural **'Hear'** (*šim'û*, 1:2; 3:1; 6:1).[4] Hence chapters 1 – 2, 3 – 5 and 6 – 7 form the primary divisions of the prophecy. Each of these divisions contains a section of judgement followed by a small, or even a larger, section proclaiming hope:

A.	1:2 – 2:13	1:2 – 2:11	=	judgement
		2:12-13	=	grace/hope
B.	3:1 – 5:15	3:1-12	=	judgement
		4:1 – 5:15	=	grace/hope
C.	6:1 – 7:20	6:1 – 7:7	=	judgement
		7:8-20	=	grace/hope

Now I am not claiming that there are no difficulties in Micah; on the contrary, there are plenty of grammatical conundrums and perplexing hermeneutical questions. But when one looks at the overall layout of the whole book, it seems to have a coherent structure. One might be forgiven for thinking this may have been *intentional*; someone with a scrap or two of intelligence must have planned it this way. And, in spite of smiles or sneers, 1:1 provides the only objective clue we have to the identity of the planner — Micah of Moresheth.[5]

Sticking with this structural breakdown and holding to the judgement-hope pattern in it, we can summarize Micah like this:

I.   Through judgement to preservation   chs. 1 – 2
II. Through judgement to peace   chs. 3 – 5
III. Through judgement to pardon   chs. 6 – 7

In order to provide more detail and a bit of a road map, let me fill in the skeleton outline above:

I. Through judgement to preservation (1:1 – 2:13)

1. The coming of the Lord (1:2-9)
2. The lament of the prophet (1:10-16)
3. The propriety of the judgement (2:1-5)
4. The problem of the preacher (2:6-11)
5. The hope for the future (2:12-13)

II. Through judgement to peace (3:1 – 5:15)

1. The approaching ruin (3:1-12)
2. The stubborn future (4:1-7)
3. The encouraging hope (4:8 – 5:5a)
4. The messianic age (5:5-15)

III. Through judgement to pardon (6:1 – 7:20)

1. The presentation of Yahweh's case (6:1-16)
2. The lamentation of Yahweh's prophet (7:1-7)
3. The endurance of Yahweh's remnant (7:8-20)

1. Through judgement to preservation

Micah 1:1 – 2:13

What, who, when
(Micah 1:1)

1:1. The word of Yahweh that came to Micah the Morashtite in the days of Jotham, Ahaz [and] Hezekiah, kings of Judah — the word he saw concerning Samaria and Jerusalem.

Here is Micah's own introduction to Micah.[1] He begins with a claim and a fact. What he is putting forth in his book is the word of Yahweh. It is not a word the prophet himself dredged up. Moreover, this word of Yahweh **'came'** to him — literally the text reads, 'the word of Yahweh that was to Micah'. That is, it was just there, present, imposing itself.[2] There is such *sovereignty* about Yahweh's word. The prophet does not control it; God presses it upon him. Yet this divine word does not shrink from using a human instrument.

The word comes to Micah the Morashtite. **'Morashtite'** refers to Micah's home town, apparently Moresheth-gath, some twenty-five miles south-west of Jerusalem, among the lowland hills of western Judah.[3]

There is mystery about Yahweh's word, then; it 'comes' or is simply 'there', and we may wonder how it comes. The only hint we have here about the 'how' is that Micah says that Yahweh's word is what he **'saw'**. This verb (*ḥāzâ*), as used here, refers to seeing in a prophetic vision (cf. Num. 24:4,16), one of the ways Yahweh conveyed his word to the prophets (cf. Num. 12:6-8); it seems to indicate that there is a visual component in the receiving of Yahweh's word which then results in the verbal communication of that word.[4] All of which relieves little of the mystery about the matter.

Our verse tells us next to nothing about Micah himself (only his previous mailing address); we are given, however, the *circumstances* in which God's word came to him: **'in the days of Jotham, Ahaz [and] Hezekiah, kings of Judah'**. Obviously this does not require us to assume that Micah prophesied from the very beginning of Jotham's reign to the very end of Hezekiah's; it only means that he prophesied during the reigns of these three kings, perhaps from about 735–700 BC. When we read 'Jotham, Ahaz, Hezekiah' we should also read another name, though it's not actually in the text — Assyria. These three kings ruled during the Assyrian decades. True, Assyrian pressure and assaults initially affected the northern kingdom (Israel) more than Micah's Judah (one thinks especially of Tiglath-pileser III's invasion in 734 BC and Shalmaneser V's clean-up of Samaria in 723-22 BC); but the big red Assyrian machine came running into Judah in 701 BC, bleeding Hezekiah's kingdom within an inch of its life.[5] In short, Micah served in fearful times. But don't miss the (ultimately) comforting word to be found here: even in scary times Yahweh does not cease bringing his word to his people.

Application

First, consider the import of 'the word of Yahweh came...' That is to say, consider *the kindness and grace of having a God who speaks and is not silent.* There is a pathetic pagan prayer in which the petitioner confesses that he does not know which god or goddess he has offended, and he does not know what sin or offence he has committed; in fact, he says, mankind as a whole wallows in this misery of agnosticism — one doesn't know whether one is committing sin or doing good.[6] How kind, then, Yahweh is, who does not allow his people to walk in darkness, but rather causes his word to come to his servant Micah, so that they will clearly know his will and his assessment of things! Grace provides clarity.

Secondly, ponder *the gratitude we owe for this digest of Micah's proclamation.* Calvin nails the point so well:

> Thus what took Micah some thirty-eight to forty years to preach, we can read within an hour. How immense our in-gratitude, then, if, seeing that Micah laboured all of his life to exhort the people of his era, and that God has so graciously provided such a brief summary of his teachings for us, we should fail to esteem them, or neglect to cast our eyes upon them.[7]

Calvin means that when church members salivate over *People* magazine and slurp up the latest titbits about Madonna or Britney Spears and yet never get to grips with the book of Micah, they are guilty of gross unthankfulness to God.

Thirdly, observe *how little detail Micah provides about himself.* It's very different from the way we bill a speaker for one of our church Bible conferences: we provide the biographical details of family, education and degrees awarded, positions held and books written. But we have none of that for Micah — only his name, date (in reference to the three kings) and postcode. That's it — nothing about his lovely wife Jeanette or his precious little Jimmy, nothing about his hobbies or how he loves apple strudel. The focus stays on the message, not the messenger — a refreshing emphasis, especially for our day, when Christians tend to fixate on their favourite evangelical gurus. 'What, after all, is Apollos? And what is Paul? Only servants, through whom you came to believe' (1 Cor. 3:5, NIV).

The bad news of the Lord's coming (Micah 1:2-9)

The passage divides itself into two main sections: first, the Lord's coming (1:2-7) and, secondly, the prophet's response (1:8-9).[8] One can break this down in more detail:

> Call to hear the Lord's testimony (1:2)
> Description of the Lord's coming (1:3-4)
> Explanation of the Lord's 'appearance' (1:5)
> Announcement of the Lord's plan (1:6-7)
> Reaction of the Lord's servant (1:8-9)

1:2
Hear, O peoples — all of them!
Pay attention, O earth, and all that fills it!
And let the Lord Yahweh be a witness against you,
    the Lord from his holy temple.

We find ourselves in a cosmic courtroom. All the **'peoples'**, throughout the whole earth, are to pay attention. The **'Lord Yahweh'** is going to bring his case against (**'be a witness against'**) the peoples of the world. Yahweh is both judge and plaintiff. His **'holy temple'** is, as in Psalm 11:4, his heavenly temple, of which the earthly temple is, we might say, a vastly scaled-down replica. Here is no ghetto deity, no mere provincial 'lordlet' of a chunk of Near-Eastern real estate. Here is the Lord of all the earth (cf. Josh. 3:11,13) summoning all the peoples of the earth to

hear his case against them. First off, the reader gets
hit between the eyes with how big Micah's God is —
'he will judge the world' (Acts 17:31; cf. Matt.
25:31-32).

1:3-4

For, see! Yahweh is coming forth from his place,
   and he shall come down
   and tread upon the high places of the earth;
and the mountains shall melt beneath him,
and the valleys will rip themselves open —
   like wax before fire,
   like waters rushing down a slope.

Yahweh is not only the witness who accuses (1:2), but
the judge who comes. That's how Micah depicts the
Lord here. His picture implies that Yahweh is neither
distant (1:3) nor safe (1:4). He is not removed, not off
somewhere in the nether reaches of the universe;
rather he comes forth, comes down, treads (1:3).
When he comes, the world seems to fall apart (1:4) —
note this effect in other texts depicting the Lord's
coming (Ps. 18:6-15; Isa. 64:1-3; Nahum 1:3-6).
   There is some debate about how all the imagery of
verse 4 fits together. But, clearly, if mountains melt
and valleys are torn up, if everything turns to hot wax
or plunging water, we have got devastation on our
hands. Micah uses such graphic language to generate
a proper *fear* of Yahweh. This is not the arrival of a
denominational committee, but the advent of the Lord
of all the earth. Our danger begins when we look at
this text and say, 'Well, now, this is symbolic language...' Maybe. But if so, symbolic of what? Symbols
point to realities. A biblical writer often uses symbolic
(or hyperbolic) language because normal description is
utterly inadequate for impressing the truth upon his
readers / hearers. Call verses 3-4 'theophanic' if it
makes you feel better, but understand that by these

verses Micah doesn't want you to feel better, but to tremble.

1:5
All this is because of the rebellion of Jacob
    and because of the sins of the house of Israel!
Who is the 'rebellion' of Jacob? Isn't it Samaria?
And who are the 'high places' of Judah? Isn't it Jerusalem?

Here Micah gives us the reason for the Lord's coming in two phrases. Both begin with the Hebrew preposition *bě*, which is frequently used in a causal sense: Yahweh is coming in judgement because of, or on account of, **'the rebellion of Jacob'** and **'the sins of the house of Israel'**. Some translations use 'transgression' for *pešaʿ*, but it is really **'rebellion'** (note the cognate verb in 2 Kings 1:1: 'Then Moab *rebelled* against Israel after Ahab died').

In the last two lines of verse 5 Micah specifies that the whole covenant people stands guilty; both the northern kingdom (**'Samaria'**) and the southern (**'Jerusalem'**) are hotbeds of rebellion and sin. He personifies these capital cities to some extent, for he asks, literally, **'Who...?'** (not 'What?'). So, if we want to identify these culprits, Micah says, **'Who is the "rebellion" of Jacob?'** and **'Who are the "high places"** [he switches to this term] **of Judah?'** He specifies the capital cities (Samaria / Jerusalem) in each case as the leading source or centre of corruption (perhaps pointing to the leadership of both nations in particular). **'High places'** were cult shrines where idolatrous and / or deviant worship was conducted (see, e.g., 1 Kings 11:7-8; 14:23-24; 2 Kings 18:4; 21:3). By equating Jerusalem with the high places of Judah, Micah implies that Jerusalem itself is one huge high place where such illegitimate worship goes on.

But we must keep verse 5 in connection with verses 2-4. Then we see what a jaw-dropping charge it is;

here Micah slams his literary fist right into the solar
plexus of his hearers. In verses 2-4 Micah is preaching
doctrine that his hearers accept without question:
Yahweh is coming to judge the world. The corollary of
this doctrine is that when the nations are judged
Israel will be delivered (see Ps. 68). Just as folk are
tempted to say 'Amen!' to Micah's preaching, he
delivers the withering punchline: **'All this'** — all this
fury and terror of the Lord's coming in judgement — is
'because of the rebellion of Jacob'; it's for the de-
pravity of Samaria and Jerusalem, the covenant
people. Prophets knew how to do this. Amos preached
repeated clips against Israel's neighbours (Amos 1:3 –
2:5), doubtless scoring huge political points with the
home team — and then he planted a leveller on Israel
(2:6-16). Later, Zephaniah begins by preaching the
Lord's announcement of worldwide judgement (Zeph.
1:2-3) only to then turn that fire hose on the people of
Judah (1:4-13). Micah does the same thing here. In
verses 2-4 he preaches the doctrine they love, the
Lord's coming, and in verse 5 he adds, 'And this is
very bad news for you.' Micah demonstrates that one
can be Yahweh's prophet and a clever communicator
at the same time.

1:6-7

And I shall make Samaria a ruin in the countryside,
    a place for planting vineyards,
and I shall heave her stones into the valley,
and I will expose her foundations.
And all her carved images will be beaten to pieces,
and her prostitutes' wages burned with fire,
and all her idols I will turn into devastating waste;
    for she collected them from the wages of a prostitute
    and they will become the wages of a prostitute again.

Here Yahweh himself speaks (note the first person: **'I
shall make Samaria a ruin...'**) and proclaims a

double devastation, for both the site (1:6) and the religion of the city (1:7). Samaria had been the pet project of kings Omri (c. 880 BC) and Ahab. It sat on an oval hilltop 300 feet high, isolated from the hills around it (except to the east), beside the ridge road running north-south, forty miles north of Jerusalem and twenty-five east of the Mediterranean[9] — an excellent defensive position, on the whole.

Yahweh will turn Samaria into a heap of ruins, with the slopes of its hill useful at least for viticulture (1:6); such slopes were prime locations for vineyards; (cf. Isa. 5:1). Yahweh will heave the stones of her walls and/or buildings into the valley below (1:6).[10] The fulfilment of Micah's prophecy may have been incremental, beginning with Samaria's fall to Assyria and Shalmaneser V in 722 BC, though only after three years of siege (see 2 Kings 17:1-6). The Babylonian Chronicle claims that Shalmaneser 'demolished' Samaria, and Sargon II, who had to recapture it about two years later, claimed to have 'rebuilt' and repopulated it.[11] More recent archaeological study suggests that physical destruction under the Assyrians may have been limited, though it is likely that the site suffered 'considerable devastation' during the time of Babylonian rule.[12] In 108/107 BC, the Hasmonean John Hyrcanus and his sons took Samaria after a year's siege, razed it to the ground, and — if Josephus is to be believed — undermined the site by tunnelling so that water, perhaps from the aqueduct, washed under the fortifications and caused their collapse.[13]

Verse 7 then depicts how Yahweh will eradicate the religion of Samaria — indeed, that of the northern kingdom. Yahweh will be venting his anger on their defiance of the first and second commandments; he does not chide them for failure to institute an urban renewal programme.

We wonder how **'prostitutes' wages'** can appear as a parallel term with **'carved images'** and **'idols'**. This may be (we are left with some guesswork) an allusion to 'sacred prostitution' and fertility rites, which permeated popular religion. A worshipper comes to the shrine, pays a fee for the services of one of the 'holy whores' on the staff and engages with her in his 'act of devotion'. Such fees may have been collected and used to purchase more images and idols. Burning the prostitutes' wages with fire may refer, then, to burning what those wages purchased — namely, more images and pagan paraphernalia.

The very last part of our verse is a puzzle. How do these items **'become the wages of a prostitute again'**? Perhaps the idea is that Samaria's conquerors will plunder the accrued funds of Samaria's shrines, take them home (to Assyria?) and use them to make more images for worshipping *their* false gods.[14] Or it may be simpler than that: the soldiers who plunder Samaria's chapels will use their loot to buy a night in a girl's bed.[15]

I think some in the democratic West find the Bible strange here. Shouldn't people have the civil liberty to worship as they please, so long as their devotion doesn't threaten others? Even if we think their worship is wrong or absurd, don't we defend their right as free persons to engage in it? If Tillie, out there on the edge of town, prays to a bowl of acorns every Thursday night, we may think *she*'s nutty, but we would say, wouldn't we, that she has a right to her religious preference? But God's people don't have that right (unless their religious preference is Yahweh). God's people live in a monarchy, not a democracy. They are not free; they are bound in covenant. They must worship Yahweh alone — or die. There's a sense in which covenant people *don't have* religious freedom.

1:8-9
Over this I will lament and wail,
I will go stripped and naked;
I will make lamentation like the jackals
    and mourning like the desert owls;
for her wounds are incurable!
Indeed! It has come all the way to Judah;
    it has reached the gate of my people,
    to Jerusalem!

Here is Micah's own reaction to his prophecy (1:8) and the reason for that reaction (1:9). He gives us both the audio (**'I will lament and wail'**) and the visual (**'I will go stripped and naked'**) versions of his response. His are not the quiet tears deemed appropriate in the West; his anguish is of the Near-Eastern, ear-splitting variety. The prophet says his lamentation is **'like the jackals'**. The jackals' howl pierces the evening or night: 'It begins with a high-pitched, long-drawn-out cry, which is repeated two or three times, each time in a higher key than before. Finally there are several short, loud, yelping barks. When one raises the cry others often join in.'[16]

Going **'stripped and naked'** may be associated with grief, but also fits the description of a captive of war who is being carted off to an unknown land (see Isa. 20). Perhaps Micah is suggesting that he is ready to act the part of an Israelite captive suffering under an Assyrian 'relocation programme'.

Why is Micah's reaction (1:8) so extreme? **'For her wounds are incurable!'** (1:9). There is no 'fix' for Samaria, no recovery; she is too far gone and can expect only the blows of Yahweh's judgement. But his anguish is aggravated because those **'wounds'** (perhaps both her sinfulness and Yahweh's judgement) are infectious — it has all **'come all the way to Judah'**.[17] Micah's own people will be ploughed under the furrows of history.

Application

This passage depicts, first, *the dark side of gospel truth* (1:2-7). Micah begins by proclaiming 'gospel doctrine' that his people would gladly accept: the Lord is coming to judge the world (1:2-4); then he turns that doctrine on them (1:5-7). The Lord will 'come' in judgement on his own professing people. They approve of the doctrine, but are oblivious to the danger. Matters can be much the same today: you may be outwardly one of God's covenant people; you may believe in the Second Coming of Jesus — you may even have definite views about his coming — and yet have no part in the blessing of that coming (cf. Amos 5:18). Jesus himself has warned us that just because we have been on the 'Jesus' band-wagon is no indication that we have a place in his kingdom (Luke 13:26-27).

This passage also shows us *the deep anguish of God's servant* (1:8-9). Micah is beside himself with grief over the catastrophe coming on Samaria and Jerusalem. Think what this shows us about a (true) prophet. A prophet is a man who fearlessly threatens God's people with God's judgement and stands against them — and then goes home and weeps shamelessly over that judgement because he cares so much for the people who are to be judged. And can we not see in Micah one greater than Micah? (See Luke 13:34-35; 19:41-44). Doesn't the prophet Jesus respond in the same way to the judgement that is coming on Jerusalem? Those who had closed their ears and eyes and hearts to him will receive what they deserve — and Jesus sobs (*klaiō*, Luke 19:41) over it. Andrew Bonar put it graphically: 'I think He will weep over the lost as He did over Jerusalem. It will be something to be said for ever in heaven, "Jesus wept as He said, Depart, ye cursed." But then it was absolutely necessary to say it.'[18] Will you be the reason for the deep anguish of God's servant Jesus?

Misery magnified
(Micah 1:10-16)

Micah doesn't simply say he will lament — he writes out his lamentation with all its word-plays and choppy grammar. I have tried to capture some of the word-plays in the translation while retaining actual place names in brackets. In an American context Micah might have said, 'Pittsburgh will be pits, Houston a hovel; Topeka will be toppled.'[19] But Micah isn't trying to be witty; he is uttering despair — and this may help to explain the difficulties and conundrums in the text. For example, the interpreter almost abandons hope of understanding verse 11.

The towns Micah mentions are in the Shephelah, the low-lying foothills to the west of the hill country of Judah, an area about twenty-seven miles long and ten miles wide.[20] The disasters the prophet foresees need not be the result of Sennacherib's ravages in about 701 BC, but could well have occurred while Ahaz ruled Judah (735–715 BC), when Syria, Israel, Edom and Philistia pummelled Judah from all sides (see 2 Chr. 28).[21]

1:10
Don't gab about it in Gath!
Don't go weeping at all!
In Dust-town [Beth-le-aphrah] roll yourself in dust!

Gath was one of the premier towns of Philistia. Scholars still debate the exact site; perhaps Tell es-Safi gets

the most votes — about twenty-five miles south-
south-east of Joppa and the same distance (as the
crow flies) west-south-west of Jerusalem.[22] Micah uses
a verb (*nāgad*, to tell) whose 'g' sound might play off of
that in 'Gath'; hence, **'Don't gab about it in Gath.'**
Micah is, I think, adapting a line from David's lament
over Saul and Jonathan in 2 Samuel 1:20. The shame
of Israel's defeat was so grievous that David, as it
were, didn't want their enemies the Philistines to hear
of it, either from Israelites or, perhaps more likely,
from ecstatic, returning Philistine warriors. It's as
though David says, 'There has been utter disaster —
let there be a media blackout.'

Micah's next line reads literally, 'Weeping, do not
weep.' The repetition of the verb root intensifies the
prohibition — i.e., **'Don't go weeping at all.'** Perhaps
the idea is that if his people give vent to their grief,
others will realize that disaster has befallen them.
They should not do anything to publish their disgrace
or to give the world a clue about the devastation of
their land.

Though word of the catastrophe that has befallen
Israel and / or Judah should be kept from enemies,
this does not mean that those who will suffer cannot
express their distress in their own locality. So the
prophet tells anyone in Beth-le-aphrah (House of
Dust, Dust-town — site unknown) to **'roll yourself in
dust'** (*'āpār*, a word-play on the town name). This was
probably a mourning rite, expressing anguish over the
crushing defeat an enemy would inflict.

1:11
Pass on for yourselves, resident of Beautyburg [Shaphir],
     in shameful nakedness!
The residents of Marchville [Zaanan] do not march forth;
lamentation in Beth-ha-ezel — its standing-place will be
     taken from you.

Here Micah ties us in grammatical and geographical knots! Geographically, he mentions three towns in this verse, and we don't know the exact location of any of them (except that they were, apparently, in the Shephelah). Grammatically, he begins with a feminine singular verb, **'Pass on'**, which agrees with the feminine singular **'resident'**, and immediately inserts a masculine plural pronoun, **'for yourselves'**. It is, I suppose, as though Micah addresses the town's population as a single representative, and yet has in view the whole lot of them at the same time. In any case, this sort of thing is not that rare.[23] (One tends to get used to it when reading Micah!)

Shaphir comes from a root meaning 'to be beautiful' — hence we could dub it **'Beautyburg'**. The catch comes in the contrast; Micah tells the resident of Beautyburg to leave town in **'shameful nakedness'**. The inhabitants may have lived in Beautyburg, but they will leave town in the opposite condition — stripped, as they are carted off as captives of war.

The place name Zaanan (ṣa'ănān) contains two letters of the verb 'to go', or 'march forth' (yāṣā'). I have tried to pick up the word-play in **'The residents of Marchville do not march forth.'** That is, they stay inside the town walls, afraid to venture out and fight the invading enemy.

The last two lines of this verse are terribly difficult. **'Lamentation in Beth-ha-ezel'** may be an exclamation. The lamentation is because the place is no more. Beth-ha-ezel could mean 'house of taking away', but one can't be sure.[24] The last line literally reads, 'He will take away from you [plural] its [or 'his'] standing-place.' This may mean that the town has no place of defence, no position from which the inhabitants can make a stand against the invaders. That would certainly be the case if the population was decimated, as the 'lamentation' implies.

1:12
To be sure, the resident of Bitterton [Maroth] longs for good,
but disaster has come down from Yahweh to the gate of
    Jerusalem.

Both lines of this verse begin with the particle *kî;* the
first one is emphatic ('indeed', or **'to be sure'**), the
second is adversative (**'but...'**), providing a contrast.
Maroth (again exact location unknown) is associated
with bitterness (cf. *mrr*, to be bitter) — hence **'Bitterton'**. Bitterton's people long for **'good'** — for help,
welfare, deliverance. However, **'disaster has come
down from Yahweh to the gate of Jerusalem'**. If
Jerusalem herself is ready to crumble, there will
surely be no help or relief for the likes of Bitterton.
'Jerusalem' comes like a thud at the end of verses
10-12, for if Jerusalem goes under the whole show is
over, the game is up for everyone. What hope can
these outlying communities have if the premier city is
herself under assault?

1:13
Hitch up the chariot to the horses [*rekesh*], resident of
    Lachish!
    It was the beginning of sin to Daughter Zion,
    for the rebellions of Israel were found in you.

We can find Lachish on the map. It is Tel ed-Duweir,
twenty-nine miles west-south-west of Jerusalem.
Lachish guarded important access routes into the
interior of the land. It was heavily fortified — during
the divided kingdom it had double defensive walls, the
upper one nineteen feet (just under six metres) thick,
the lower thirteen (four metres). When Sennacherib
finally took Lachish in around 701 BC, he took up
seventy linear feet (over twenty-one metres) of his
palace wall to depict his conquest.[25] (What else could
he do? He had failed to conquer Jerusalem.)

There is a sound-play between **'horses'** (*rekesh*) and **'Lachish'**. Had Micah been in Scotland he might have urged, 'Hop on the train, you residents of Tain.' The Lachishites, however, are not hitching chariots to horses in order to fight, but to flee. They should get out of town before the enemy assaults them. Sadly, the prophet accuses Lachish of being infectious — she had apparently embraced the **'rebellions of Israel'**, the twisted, syncretistic worship of the northern kingdom, and then became a conduit that transmitted this corrupt worship into the life of the southern kingdom. I take **'Israel'** here as referring to the northern kingdom.[26]

1:14
Therefore you will give parting gifts to Moresheth-gath;
the houses of Deceitville [Achzib] have proven deceitful
    to the kings of Israel.

Moresheth-gath seems to be the full name of Micah's home town (see 1:1), located six miles north-east of Lachish. The verb form, **'you will give'** (or 'you must give'), is feminine singular. Some think it refers to 'Daughter Zion', i.e., Jerusalem, in verse 13. However, it could just as well refer to Lachish. Since the people of Lachish want to make a quick getaway to avoid their attackers, they certainly cannot expect their satellite towns like Moresheth-gath to stick with them; they might just as well dismiss them and allow them to do their best on their own.

The word for **'parting gifts'** is used two other times in the Old Testament. The first is in Exodus 18:2, where it seems to mean 'dismissal' — i.e., Moses sends his wife back to her father's house while the furore in Egypt is heating up. The second is in 1 Kings 9:16, where Pharaoh gave Gezer, which he had conquered, to his daughter as a wedding gift when she became Solomon's wife. In any case, Lachish must release Moresheth-gath, either to be on her own or to be given over to another (in this case, not to a husband, but to an invader).[27] In the second part of verse 14 Micah plays on the town name Achzib (from *kāzab*, to lie; hence, **'Deceitville'**) — it has proven *'akzāb* (deceptive, disappointing), and this to **'the kings of Israel'**. This last phrase really has the commentators scratching their heads. Many hold that when Micah says **'Israel'** he really means 'Judah', since they assume that Micah's lament is primarily connected to Sennacherib's devastation of Judah in 701 BC, some years after the northern kingdom had ceased to exist. But if Micah's lament takes in both Samaria and Jerusalem (see 1:1,5-6), it might well encompass all that is going to take place from, say, 735 BC onwards, and might therefore include Assyria's strangulation of Israel, as well as the pummelling of Judah to within an inch of its life by Israel and Syria (see introductory comments to 1:10-16 on page 29). If so — and obviously this is a conjecture — Judah could have been forced to cede territory to Israel, including Moresheth-gath and Achzib; but the prophet may be saying that such 'victories' are empty, nothing Israel's kings can hang their hats on, because the big Assyrian nation-smasher is going to chew up Israel and spit her out.[28]

1:15

I will again bring the conqueror to you, resident of Conquest
    [Mareshah];
the glory of Israel will come all the way to Adullam.

The first-person verb, **'I will ... bring'**, assumes that Yahweh is speaking. The threat is against Mareshah, Tell Sandakhanna, about four miles east-north-east of Lachish and two miles south of Moresheth-gath (1:14). There is a word or sound-play between the root for **'conqueror'** (*yāraš*) and the town name Mareshah;

hence the translation, **'I will bring the conqueror to you, resident of Conquest.'** Mareshah will go the way of all her sister towns; a victor will conquer Victory.

The **'glory of Israel'** in the second line could refer to Yahweh (cf. Jer. 2:11) coming to inflict judgement, or to the king, or people who are 'upper-class' citizens (cf. Isa. 5:13, where 'glory' = 'men of rank,' NIV) coming to seek refuge — probably the latter. Adullam was east-north-east of Moresheth-gath and twelve to thirteen miles west-south-west of Bethlehem. In his outlaw days David used a cave near Adullam as a hideout for himself and his ragtag outfit (cf. 1 Sam. 22:1-2). Micah may see an ironic twist here: as David once had to run for his life to Adullam, now Israel's high-ranking citizens become refugees, fleeing to David's place because their country is going down the drain. **'Israel'** may well mean the northern kingdom here; see comments on verse 14.[29]

1:16
Make yourself bald, shave your head over the sons you dote
     over!
Make your baldness like the vulture's,
     for they have gone from you into exile.

Finally, Micah probably calls on Mother Jerusalem (the imperatives are feminine singulars) to mourn over the tragedy of her children (the population throughout Judah). Israel was forbidden to practise pagan mourning rites that involved ritualized shaving of the head (Deut. 14:1); however, as here, some shaving of the head was allowable, or even ordered, as an appropriate sign of anguish and mourning (Isa. 22:12; Jer. 7:29; Ezek. 7:18; cf. Amos 8:10).[30] In fact, Jerusalem was to shear her own head over her beloved children, leaving it as bald as the griffon-vulture's appears to be — its head is covered with short, creamy down which looks bare from a distance.[31]

Her anguish is because her children **'have gone ...
into exile'** from her. Micah, in his prophetic vision,
sees these deportations as having already taken place.
The reference to **'exile'** need not point to the Babylonian exile(s), for the Assyrians were in the habit of
carting off populations and relocating them.

Application

Let's say a married couple lives in a downstairs apartment or flat.
The husband comes home early from work one day to find that a
plumbing fiasco has occurred in the apartment above them and
their whole apartment has caught the overflow — three rooms and
almost all they contain are sopping wet. He thinks, momentarily,
that he will jump in, begin to clean up the disaster; he can at least
make a dent in the recovery operation. Then he decides against
that — no, he will leave it all just as he found it; his wife must be
able to see exactly how awful it is. It needs to hit her in the same
way it has hit him.

One wonders if Micah made that kind of decision here. The
word- and sound-plays show that, from a human standpoint, he
gave careful thought to how he would express the ravaging that
was coming on Judah. And yet he didn't 'clean it up' — i.e., he
didn't polish up the diction and correct all the grammatical anoma-
lies that litter his lament.[32] So Micah leaves it in the rough draft, so
that we can sense his own anguish and see what a savage
disaster Yahweh's judgement is going to inflict. 'Here in 1:10-16
we seem to have the raw product, straight from the soul of the
prophet, who could not restrain the torrent of words (or sounds) —
an almost incoherent speech forced from his lips by the Spirit of
God.'[33]

Micah said he would lament and wail (1: 8), and this (1:10-16)
is it. He wants Jerusalem to respond in a frenzy of anguish (1:16)
which might lead to repentance. At the same time, recording his
own torment fulfils part of his prophetic vocation of grieving over
Yahweh's judgement falling on Yahweh's people (cf. Amos 7:1-6;
Jer. 14:7-9,19-22; Ezek. 9:8; 11:13).

The prophet should be a model for us. Far too often divine judgement is a doctrine we affirm rather than a reality we abhor. We have far too little of the prophet's agony. He wailed over a people who had the Scriptures and their promises, who had known the works and deliverances of God and who were turning their back on it all. I think of the analogous situation in western European and North American culture. People who have enjoyed the light of the Scriptures, the fruit of the Reformation and the revivals now choose to walk by the light of their own darkness, and the hands of millions slide down the slimy sides of the bottomless pit. We can write books about the phenomenon, chart its course, uncover its causes, but we too seldom ever grieve over the tragedy. There are also sections of the church that disdain to follow a 'close reading' of the Bible and plunge into doctrinal indifference and (not surprisingly) moral anarchy (witness the hue and cry among some for approval and sanction of same-sex 'unions'). It is easy for us to bemoan the trend, to shake our heads, but few of us pour out a torrent of agony and despair before the One who has been rejected.

Sovereign schemer
(Micah 2:1-5)

Notice the way this passage (2:1-5) breaks down:

Crime (2:1-2)
Retribution:
    Therefore — disaster (2:3-4)
    Therefore — exclusion (2:5)

So here Micah denounces wrong (2:1-2) and announces judgement (2:3-5). Let's pick apart the text.

2:1-2
Woe to those scheming wickedness
    and executing disaster upon their beds!
At morning light, they do it,
    because it is in the power of their hand.
They covet fields — and seize them,
and they covet houses — and take them;
they put the squeeze on a man and his household,
    yes, a man and his possession.

The prophet roasts those who plot their wickedness in advance and then execute it (2:1), using force to do so (2:2). Their conduct is clearly premeditated (2:1); note **'covet'** (2:2). Micah says they even lie awake at night, **'upon their beds'** (2:1), scheming how to get richer; then they pull it off when they go to the real-estate office and the court the next day (2:1). If someone asks them why they do this, they retort:

'Because we can' (for the idiom, **'in the power of
their hand'**, see Gen. 31:29; Deut. 28:32; Prov. 3:27;
Neh. 5:5).
But what was their wickedness? Verse 2 spells it
out. They were amassing land and property (**'fields'**
and **'houses'**; cf. Isa. 5:8). They 'seized' fields; the
verb is *gāzal*, to take by force — it is likely that physical violence was involved.[34] One can imagine these
people turning up with eviction papers that had the
stamp of the local governing authority on them. Their
actions were heartless but 'legal'.[35] Verses 8-9 indicate that widows and dependent children may have
been their special prey. A husband / father may have
died leaving a debt, and so these sharks move in to
foreclose on the loan. However, these crooks were
magnanimous — they didn't simply pick on women
and children, but went after the landowners as well:
'they put the squeeze on [traditionally, 'oppressed'] **a
man and his household, yes, a man and his possessions'** (2:2). Bruce Waltke captures the trouble
well:

> In that agrarian economy a person's life de-
> pended on his fields, and for that reason his in-
> heritance was carefully safeguarded by the Law.
> It was a sacred trust, not just another piece of
> real estate. If a person lost his fields, at best he
> might become a day labourer; at worst, he might
> become a slave. In either case he lost his inde-
> pendence, his freedom before God, and became a
> dependent of the land barons.[36]

1 Kings 21 shows us long before Micah's day how
helpless a man could be when the government decided
it wanted his inheritance. Note that in Micah 1 men
distort worship (1:5,7,9); here in chapter 2 they despise people. One suspects a connection.

2:3-5
Therefore, here is what Yahweh says:
'See! I am scheming disaster against this family;
you will not withdraw your necks from it,
and you will not walk around arrogantly,
    for it will be disaster time.
On that day one will take up a piece of sarcasm against you
    and utter a dire lament:
one will say,
    "We are totally wasted;
    he takes away my people's portion;
    how he removes what is mine;
    how he doles out our fields to the rebellious!"
Therefore you will have no one throwing the line
    for a share of land in the assembly of Yahweh.'

Here is Yahweh's announcement of judgement, and
we must not miss his fine word-play. He begins with,
'See! I am scheming disaster against this family'
(2:3). Micah had already used this terminology when
he introduced the unscrupulous characters in verse 1:
they were 'scheming' (*ḥāšab*) wickedness and carrying
out 'disaster' (*rāʿ*) on others as they hatched their
night-time schemes. So Yahweh uses the same lingo,
indicating that he will repay them in kind: 'I am
scheming disaster against this family.' The sovereign
schemer will go to work!

What sort of **'disaster'** is he devising?

It is an *unavoidable* disaster: **'you will not withdraw your necks from it'** (2:3). Yahweh pictures
these suave wheeler-dealers as farm draught animals,
slapped into a yoke and unable to release themselves.

And it is *humiliating*: **'you will not walk around
arrogantly, for it will be disaster time'** (2:3). Yahweh's scourge will knock the strut out of their step.

Verse 4 underscores how *appropriate* Yahweh's
judgement will be. Here we need to go into slow mo-
tion, since this verse sports its own set of difficulties.

It begins by saying that **'one'** (the verb is impersonal) **'will take up a piece of sarcasm against you'** (the pronoun is plural — a reference to the real-estate crooks). The Hebrew *māšāl* does not always indicate sarcasm or ridicule; it can simply mean a proverb or saying, but in certain contexts it takes on a 'nastier' hue (see Isa. 14:4; Hab. 2:6). Here it is certainly coloured by the next clause, **'utter a dire lament'**. Literally, this last clause reads: 'And one shall lament a lamentation, a lamentation' — a verb followed by two cognate nouns, one masculine, one feminine.[37] The repetition is probably emphatic and indicates a most dire or excruciating lament or groaning. Then Micah quotes the lamentable lament; he signals that he is doing so by using the verb *'āmar*, 'one says', or **'one will say'**, and then the sad piece follows:

> **We are totally wasted;**
> **he takes away my people's portion;**
> **how he removes what is mine;**
> **how he doles out our fields to the rebellious!**

The **'we'** I take to be the former land tycoons of Judah who had amassed their estates by filching the holdings of others. The **'he'** refers primarily to Yahweh (cf. Calvin). They lament that God **'removes what is mine'** — that is, the land and estates that have become theirs because they preyed on other people and swallowed up their land and homes. In the last line they seem incredulous that Yahweh would hand over **'our fields'** to pagans, of all people! So Micah has written their script, puts it in their mouths and allows them to mock themselves — as if to say, 'Oh, yes, such a pity, so unpleasant, that you should suffer the loss of *your* turf, as you call it.'[38]

Finally, Micah says Yahweh's disaster will be *frightening*: **'you will have no one throwing the line for a share of land in the assembly of Yahweh'** (2:5). The

'line' is a measuring line, which, in its extended
meaning, designates a measured portion of land. One
sees this in Joshua 18:1-10, where Joshua casts lots
for seven tribes to determine what chunks of land they
will receive as an inheritance. In our verse Micah
speaks to any one of these land-sharks he has been
giving a dressing-down[39] and tells him that he will
have no part in the future reassignment of the land.
There is a gleam of hope in verse 5. The land may be
handed over to the rebellious (2:4), but the time will
come when Yahweh's people will gather once again to
parcel out the land among themselves.[40] However,
these land-grubbers will have no part in it. They will
be cut off from Yahweh's people. That is meant to be
frightening. Micah says in effect that they 'have neither part nor lot in this matter' (cf. Acts 8:21).

Application

Many Christians would probably admit that this section leaves
them cold, since Micah condemns the rich and powerful here and,
as few Christians find themselves in that category — well then, this
passage has little to say to them. If that is your view, cheer up!
Micah nails you after all! You may have neither position nor power
to pull off this sort of white-collar crime. But Micah takes you down,
down, behind the obvious crimes to their secret root: 'They covet'
(2:2). The prophet takes you beneath all the layers to the really
ugly stuff.

   John Guy writes of the surprise people received at the execution of Mary Queen of Scots in 1587. As the executioner lifted up
Mary's head (after clumsily severing it) her auburn curls and white
cap became detached from her skull. The executioner was left
with a fistful of hair, while Mary's head fell back to the floor and
began rolling like an odd-shaped ball towards the gathered spec-
tators — who saw that it was very grey and nearly bald.[41] Get
beneath the wig and you see what the queen really looked like at
the age of forty-four.

Micah is not sneezing at flagrant sins, but he also strips away those trimmings and takes you to their source, the idolatrous passion of the human heart: 'They covet.'[42] Here is a God who can see it — what you ponder in your bedroom (2:1), the secret plans you make and the raging discontentment at the core of your life that drives it all. The fact that you have done nothing like the thugs in the text does not mean you are virtuous, but only that you may lack opportunity to sin in this way. With that verb 'covet' Yahweh opens up the septic tank of your own reeking nature and lets you smell it.

Preachers are problems
(Micah 2:6-11)

It seems there are no easy texts in the prophecy of Micah. This passage (2:6-11) only proves the rule. Not to scare you, but one major commentary takes almost forty pages to discuss these six verses. One should not ignore difficulties; however, difficulties should not take over our study to such an extent that they break up or obscure the flow of the text. Let's see if we can keep that balance. For a summary, then, I would propose that here you can see the prophet, firstly, facing the pressure (2:6-7), secondly, reaffirming the truth (2:8-10) and then, thirdly, using some sarcasm (2:11).

2:6-7
'Don't preach' is what they preach.
They will not preach about these things;
disgraces will not depart.
Should it be said, O house of Jacob,
    'Is the Spirit of Yahweh losing patience?'
    Or, 'Are these his doings?'
Do not my words bring good
    to the one who walks uprightly?

Micah says that his opponents preach about preaching.[43] **'Don't preach'** is a plural verb — hence the prohibition is directed against Micah and his fellow prophets who preach a similar message. Some translations also take the rest of the verse to be the words of Micah's opponents; hence the NRSV of verse 6:

'Do not preach' — thus they preach —
'one should not preach of such things;
disgrace will not overtake us.'

The NIV and CSB are similar. But the second line is
not modal or subjunctive ('should not'); the Hebrew
seems to be a straightforward indicative: **'They will
not preach about these things.'** This, then, is Micah's criticism of his critics. They want to stifle his
preaching of judgement, and they themselves wouldn't
be caught dead preaching such a negative message!
The phrase **'these things'** refers to the disasters
Yahweh threatens in verses 3-5.

The last line of verse 6 is tough. Contrary to the
interpretation of the NRSV etc., I take it as Micah's
comment (cf. NASB): **'disgraces will not depart'** —
i.e., since Micah's opponents will not preach warning
and judgement, there is no way the nation can avoid
disgrace and disaster. However, the line is a conundrum: the word for **'disgraces'** (*kĕlimmôt*) is feminine
plural, while the verb **'depart'** (*yissag*) is masculine
singular. One would prefer better grammatical agree-
ment than that! There are, however, other cases of
this.[44]

In verse 7 the prophet quotes two questions that the
people of Judah kept asking — it was their way of
objecting to Micah's message of judgement: **'Is the
Spirit of Yahweh losing patience?'** (as if to say, 'I
thought Yahweh was long-suffering, slow to anger,
Micah? So now are you saying he is going to act in a
way that is contrary to his declared nature and zap us
with judgement?'); **'Are these his doings?'** By **'these'**
they refer to the disasters threatened in verses 3-5. So
they ask, 'Are those the kind of things we would expect
from a God who has promised to make goodness and
mercy follow us all the days of our lives? Will Yahweh's
"from everlasting-to-everlasting" steadfast love throw
us into the frying pan all of a sudden?' In response to

this barrage Micah leaves it to Yahweh to pose his own
question: **'Do not my words bring good to the one
who walks uprightly?'** In other words, enjoyment of
covenant benefits only comes to those who are faithful
in keeping covenant stipulations (cf. Deut. 11:26-28).
Why should those who despise God's word expect to
receive God's goodness? (cf. Jer. 7:5-15).

Verses 6-7 depict the duress that Micah and genuine prophets were under. The pseudo-prophets were
not about to preach judgement: **'They will not
preach about these things'** (2:6). The pressure was
on to speak only the 'smooth' word (see Isa. 30:9-11).
One can almost hear one of Micah's critics giving him
a dressing-down: 'This threatening of judgement isn't
like our merciful covenant God. Micah, don't you
remember, as the hymn says, "There's a wideness in
God's mercy"? And remember that pop song from
years back? "Though it makes him sad to see the way
we live, he'll always say, 'I forgive.'" You won't win
anyone by fear. You're still standing at Sinai, Micah,
and have never come to know God as your Friend.
You're going to give people the idea that God is some
nasty, fire-breathing ogre. Why, I couldn't bring myself
to believe in a God like that.' In short, there is no
market for Micah's message. And yet when there is
such insistence on always proclaiming the love of God,
the blessing of God, the comfort of God, one has the
odd feeling that something is being manipulated.

2:8
But lately my people rise up as an enemy;
you strip off the robe from the clothes
    — from those who pass by trustingly
    [like] ones returning from war.

In verses 8-10 Micah reasserts his message, with its
charges (2:8-9) and consequences (2:10). He is probably quoting Yahweh's words — the double **'my**

people' (2:8,9) hints at this (note 'my words' in the last line of verse 7).

In verse 8 Yahweh depicts his people acting like their enemies and inflicting wrong on fellow Judeans. The phrase translated **'strip off the robe'** involves a little guesswork. The word in the text is masculine (*'eder*) and means 'splendour', but if a final 't' is added (which may have been omitted by accident since the next word begins with 't' — a little problem called haplography) it becomes feminine and sometimes means 'robe' or 'cloak'. The picture is that of pillage wreaked on otherwise unsuspecting folk (**'those who pass by trustingly'**).

The last phrase of verse 8 is a puzzle. Literally, it reads, **'ones returning from war'**. What is the picture? One possibility is to take the line quite closely with **'you strip off'**. They fleece their fellow citizens of practically everything, so that the latter resemble a defeated army returning home; the enemy has divested them of everything except life.[45]

2:9
You drive out the women of my people
    from their pleasant houses;
from their children you take away my splendour for ever.

Verse 9 describes the real-estate takeovers: **'You drive out the women of my people.'** These may be women who have been widowed, and so are without male protection; we don't have enough detail to fill out the whole picture. But these are not (or *were* not) destitute ladies — they have (or rather had) **'pleasant'**, comfortable homes.[46] The land-grabbers are not messing around sucking up the miserable hovels of the poor, but going after the fine homes of those with some property and means. They make these eviction notices count for something worth obtaining. In doing this they also **'take away my splendour for ever'** from the children in these homes. Yahweh's **'splen-dour'** here is the gift of a splendid land that should in the normal course of events be inherited by one's descendants.[47] But when these samples of scum seize houses and property from the (widowed?) mothers they at the same time divest the children of their rightful future.

2:10
Get up and go off!
For this is not the resting-place,
    because it is defiled;
    it will bring ruin — a sickening ruin at that.

Now Yahweh, or Micah, announces the consequences for these things: **'Get up and go off!'** Waltke very plausibly suggests that the order may be loaded with irony. These may be the very words these real-estate 'developers' had spoken when they evicted women and children from their rightful homes.[48] Now they them-selves must vacate the land, for it is not the **'resting-place'** (cf. Deut. 12:9; Ps. 95:11) it was meant to be, because it has been **'defiled'** by their crimes. Micah gives a moral twist to a ceremonial word ('defiled'),[49] indicating how their thuggery has polluted the land. What should have brought rest will instead **'bring ruin — a sickening ruin at that'**.

2:11
If a wind-bag goes around and utters lies:
    'I will preach to you of wine and beer!'
— he shall be the preacher for this people!

Now Micah mixes prophecy with sarcasm as he sketches what it takes to be a 'popular' preacher in Judah. He seems to dabble in double meanings as he begins, 'If a man goes around a *rûaḥ*'. He probably means 'as a *rûaḥ*'. The word can mean both 'spirit' and 'wind'. Micah may be implying that these pseudo-prophets who go around claiming to be men of the *Spirit* (with the Spirit of God directing their prophecy) are really nothing but *wind*. They are simply windbags.[50] And they 'utter lies' (literally, 'he lies a falsehood'). The term for **'lies'**, or 'falsehood', is *šeqer*; his word for **'beer'**, or 'liquor', in the next line, is *šēkār*, and Micah may want us to divine a word-play. Of course, it is hard to anglicize. A rough attempt might be: 'He utters falsehood and preaches Falstaff.'

Micah hits out at the purveyors of the 'prosperity gospel'. If a fellow promises, **'I will preach to you of wine and beer,'** why, the prophet mocks, that is just the sort of preacher these people want. **'Wine and beer'** probably point to the blessings of the covenant (cf. Lev. 26:3-5,9-10; Deut. 28:2-6,8,11), and when these windbags preach their positive message, their hearers drink it up. They love to hear the covenant promises, but not the covenant prescriptions; they like its comforts, but not its commandments. They assume that a prophet's function is to tell them what they want to hear: that the barometer is rising, the economy is expanding and God is smiling.

Application

When the Nazis held Germany in their clutches, they dismissed Helmut Thielicke, among others, from his university lectureship. Thielicke eventually managed to protest against his dismissal before the so-called National Head of Lecturers in Munich — to no avail. As the mighty lackey told him, 'As long as theology faculties exist ... I will make sure that only sucking pigs and no wild boars are appointed to professorships.'[51] At least he had the gift of clarity. That is still the pressure; people, the culture and, sometimes, the church prefer sucking pigs. They want to control the messengers and so control the message. Even church gurus will insist that we should have no negativism in our message —

no guilt, no wrong, no justice, no judgement. We must not make people feel bad about themselves. But then the cross becomes a charade, for then there is no wrath of God that falls upon the Son of God, who took my hell as his portion. If you do not hear of your sin, your guilt, your ruin, how can the cross of Christ become the shelter of Christ from those very curses? But the current preference is to hear of the bland benevolence of a non-existent, spineless deity.

But this pressure on Christ's servants reaches beyond the public proclamation of the word. Sometimes one finds it in a very private arena. For example, a pastor has just been told by a church member that he hopes the pastor will agree to officiate at his daughter's wedding, even though she was previously divorced on non-biblical grounds. If he refuses, the member will, of course, be very upset and leave the church and, since the church is not large, this would adversely affect the pastor's salary. Ah, the life of a wild boar is hard!

Waiting for 'the Breaker'
(Micah 2:12-13)

Not even Calvin could believe it. Here Micah seems to hold open a window of hope after having closed up his hearers to a barrage of judgement. But for Calvin the change was too abrupt; he could not see how Micah could change his tune so suddenly. Hence he took 2:12-13 as more of the same: the Lord was 'gathering' his people for destruction and their king would be going 'before them' into captivity.[52] Others, who also think the shift from blight to blessing too abrupt, have decided that Micah is quoting the 'positive prophets' he has just attacked in verse 11 — i.e., verses 12-13 are their empty promise of the 'victorious life'. But that will hardly wash. These verses assume that the people have been scattered or dispersed or confined (otherwise, why would they need to be 'gathered'?) — something the 'positive' prophets would not admit to be possible (cf. 2:6-7).[53] So these verses are a word of hope even though that is surprising after the torrent of judgement. (I will deal with the 'problem' of hope in the face of judgement when we come to Micah 4.) In my overview of the prophecy I characterized chapters 1-2 as 'through judgement to preservation'. Verses 12-13 speak of the preservation.

Notice the scheme for this text. Verse 12 is in the first person as direct address from Yahweh; verse 13 is in the third person as an 'explanation' or expansion from the prophet. Gathering in safety is the key image in verse 12; liberation from confinement is the primary picture in verse 13.

2:12
'I will surely gather Jacob — all of you;
I will surely collect the remnant of Israel;
I will place them together like sheep of Bozrah,
    like a flock in the middle of its pasture;
they will be noisy because of the people.'

Yahweh's address begins with two first-person 'imperfect' verb forms, each preceded by a cognate infinitive. The construction underscores the sureness of the action: **'I will surely gather... I will surely collect...'** This then is a *certain* hope. At the same time it is a *distant* one, for, as Keil says, 'the assembling together presupposes a dispersion among the heathen, such as Micah had threatened' (1:11,16; 2:4).[54] We can set no dates; but at least the 'regathering' is a long way down the road chronologically and is not something about to occur in the near future.

The regathering includes **'Jacob — all of you'**. **'Jacob'** refers to the whole twelve-tribe people. However, in the next line Yahweh more narrowly defines what he means by all of Jacob, namely, the **'remnant of Israel'**. The thought may be that Jacob / Israel will be reduced to a remnant by Yahweh's judgement.[55] So here is a *selective* or restricted hope. There is an assumption beneath the text that being a genetic Israelite is no automatic ticket to a place among God's preserved people. After all, in Romans 9:6 Paul was not announcing a new discovery but repeating an acknowledged principle.

The second half of verse 12 gives a picture of what the 'gathering' looks like. Literally it reads, 'I will place him together like sheep of Bozrah.' It is likely that the singular 'him' is used for the plural **'them'**. Bozrah was a city in northern Edom, astride the caravan route, about twenty-five miles south-east of the southern tip of the Dead Sea. However, the term could be a common noun, meaning an enclosure or pen. This latter possibility would more easily depict the sheep's security, along with the next phrase, **'like a flock in the middle of its pasture'**. It's the last clause that is more baffling. The **'they'** in **'they will be noisy'** is feminine, perhaps taking in both **'sheep'** (feminine) and **'flock'** (masculine). The verb suggests uproar or confusion,[56] which could be positive or negative depending on one's point of view. I take the preposition *min* prefixed to 'man / men' as causal and so construe the text as saying that they will be noisy, or in an uproar, 'because of men' — i.e., because of the huge number of people Yahweh gathers and restores. The NBV captures it nicely: 'it will be humming with people'. I assume the thought to be akin to that of Ezekiel 36:37-38. If so, we also have a *substantial* hope, since, though somewhat paradoxically the hope is restricted to a 'remnant', it will nevertheless be a very sizeable remnant!

2:13
The Breaker shall go up before them;
they shall break out,
   so that they pass through the gate and go out by it;
their king passes on before them,
   even Yahweh at their head.

Now the prophet fleshes out Yahweh's promise with additional explanation. The promise, he implies, holds out a *liberating* hope. The picture seems to depict confinement, perhaps in a city (note the reference to a **'gate'**). But one called **'the Breaker'** goes up before his people; they in turn **'break out ... pass through the gate and go out by it'**. 'Breaker' is a participle of the verb *pāraṣ*, which is then used again of the people — they 'break out'.

The verb conjures up an episode from David's conflicts with the Philistines. David used this very verb to describe Yahweh's victory over the Philistines in 2 Samuel 5:20, where the *prṣ*-root occurs four times (the 's' usually being anglicized as a 'z'):

> So David came to Baal-*perazim*, and David struck them down there and said, 'Yahweh has *broken through* my enemies before me like an *outbursting* of waters.' Therefore he called the name of that place Baal-*perazim*.

'Baal-perazim' means 'lord of burstings out' — David's way of remembering how Yahweh had burst out against and broken down the Philistines. Yahweh's activity, he said, was like a massive torrent of water levelling everything in its path.[57] That is what Micah's *pōrēṣ* does here — he smashes and breaks down whatever holds, confines, or imprisons his people.

In the second part of verse 13 Micah portrays the procession of the freed people: **'their king passes on before them, even Yahweh at their head'**. I take the conjunction attached to **'Yahweh'** as having a specifying function; in other words, it means 'that is'. Yahweh is not someone in addition to **'their king'**; rather he *is* their king. This sheds light on the identity of the 'Breaker'. On the one hand, **'the Breaker shall go up before them'**; on the other, **'their king [=Yahweh] passes on before them'**. The parallel associates or identifies the Breaker with the king/Yahweh. It looks as though 'Breaker' is Micah's nickname for the divine Messiah.[58] Hence we also have a *personal* hope here. And we should not miss the fact that he 'shall go up before them' and 'passes on before them'; it indicates that he both smashes and stays, that he both liberates and leads.[59] He is not a deliverer just for the moment of need, but for the long haul.

How are we to understand the fulfilment of this passage? Some tie verses 12-13 to Yahweh's deliverance of Jerusalem from the Assyrian siege in 701 BC (2 Kings 18 – 19).⁶⁰ Refugees from Judah poured into Jerusalem; the besieged city looked as though it would become a huge gas chamber operated by the Assyrians, but Yahweh devastated the Assyrian troops in their sleeping bags one night, and Jerusalem was delivered. I am not persuaded. For one thing, the image in verse 13 does not seem to fit Jerusalem when it says the Breaker will **'go up'** (*'ālâ*); as Wolff says, this cannot refer to Jerusalem, 'for upon departing from the city, one goes down, not up'.⁶¹ I tend to think the prophecy is broader and less specific than that. I much prefer Keil's view:

> The fulfilment of this prophecy commenced with the gathering together of Israel to its God and King by the preaching of the gospel, and will be completed at some future time when the Lord shall redeem Israel, which is now pining in dispersion, out of the fetters of its unbelief and life of sin.⁶²

Application

If you had to wend your way through the dangerous streets of a large city at night, and if you had a choice between two companions, whom would you choose — Manfred or Rocky? Why would you choose Rocky? Isn't it because the very name connotes virility and toughness? And what if you have a Messiah whose name is 'Breaker' or 'Smasher'? It's really quite steadying. And what he brings about is unstoppable. Hengstenberg highlighted this note of power in our text: 'The three verbs, "they break through", "they march through", "they go out", describe in a pictorial manner progress which cannot be stopped by any human power.'⁶³

Such a note reminds me of a fascinating minister in the Scottish Highlands in the 1700s. Aeneas Sage was a man of enormous strength, and he found that kind invitations to worship did not work with the people in his parish. They were keen for games, but not for God, on the sabbath. Sage had challenged and then thrown the champion wrestler for the area, Big Rory. Rory took his defeat in good heart and willingly entered into an alliance with the minister. Come the next sabbath, when the locals were at their games, Sage and Big Rory sallied forth; each grabbed a couple of men, dragged them to the chapel, locked them in — and kept repeating the ploy until they had a respectable captive congregation. Big Rory stood at the back brandishing a club in case someone decided he was not interested in worship. Mr Sage then ascended the pulpit, led worship and preached.[64] The fascinating thing is that there was such inevitability about it. Sage wanted a sabbath congregation; he was going to have one — and there was nothing anyone was going to do to stop it.

That is the 'feel' that this part of Micah's prophecy gives. If the Messiah is 'Breaker' or 'Smasher', and if he is bent on gathering and liberating his people, what, or who, can possibly stand in his way? And doesn't that put grit into your soul and steel into your bones?

2. Through judgement to peace
Micah 3:1 – 5:15

Rush to ruin
(Micah 3:1-12)

With chapter 3 we enter a new division of Micah's prophecy, which I have dubbed 'through judgement to peace'. This division covers chapters 3 – 5 and breaks, as do the other divisions, into a section of judgement (3:1-12) followed by one of grace or hope (4:1 – 5:15). In the next few pages we study the judgement section.

And I want to take all of chapter 3 together. It would be more digestible to swallow its three sections separately, but I think we would lose the unity and overall punch of the chapter that way. Note then that two sections, the first and third (3:1-4 and 3:9-12), primarily address leaders and rulers, while the middle one (3:5-8) concerns the prophets. In each section the last verse (3:4,8,12) contains the punchline or contrast. We might summarize chapter 3 this way: Micah accuses the civil and religious leadership of particular *perversions* and announces certain *deprivations* that will be inflicted because of those perversions. Hence we can divide the text up as follows:

1. Perversion of responsibility (3:1-4)
   Therefore, no rescue;
              the eclipse of Yahweh's help

2. Perversion of proclamation (3:5-8)
    Therefore, no revelation;
        the eclipse of Yahweh's word

3. Perversion of promises (3:9-12)
    Therefore, no temple;
        the eclipse of Yahweh's kingdom

Now on to the text.

3:1-3
Then I said:
Hear now, leaders of Jacob and rulers of the house of
    Israel —
Aren't you the ones who are supposed to know justice?
Haters of good and lovers of evil,
who rip their skin off of them
and their flesh from their bones,
and who eat the flesh of my people,
strip their skin off them,
smash up their bones,
chop them up like something in a kettle
    and like meat in a cooking pot.

Downtown Jerusalem, 3.00 a.m. Imagine a lone figure
struggling along; he lugs a small sledgehammer and a
newly-painted placard on a chunk of half-inch ply-
wood to which he has nailed two stakes. He drags his
cargo across the small lawn until he is right in front of
the squat stone sign that identifies the building as the
'Hall of Justice'. He positions his sign, hammers in the
stakes with his sledge and walks away. Five hours
later Judah's civil servants arrive for work and read:

Jerusalem stockyards — best butchers in town;
    we slaughter, skin, slice and serve!

That is essentially what Micah has done in verses 1-3. He addresses Judah's civil magistrates, the **'leaders'** (literally, 'heads') and **'rulers'**, in verse 1 and then lays into them about their duty (3:1), affections (3:2) and practices (3:2-3). He is not addressing the land barons of 2:1-2, but the magistrates who provide the legal 'cover' for such nasty pieces of work.[1] It is their calling to **'know justice'** — i.e., to carry out their duty in maintaining 'a right order' by making and enforcing equitable legal decisions (Deut. 1:15-17) in line with God's covenant law (cf. Exod. 21 – 23).[2] To 'know justice', remember, means more than having a thorough acquaintance with the law and a superb legal research library. It is like Yahweh's 'knowing' the way of the righteous in Psalm 1:6 — a preoccupied concern, a close interest, a protective care. To 'know justice' means it is 'in your blood' to see it done and established.

These fellows do anything but that — which is hardly surprising, however, considering their disposition as **'haters of good and lovers of evil'** (3:2). So Micah reserves his best sarcasm for these butchers. They rip the skin off their victims; in fact, they are so thorough that they take off the flesh right down to the bone (3:2). In verse 3 he depicts the whole process of the cannibals' cuisine: they strip off the skin, smash up the bones and chop it up like something for the cauldron or like hunks of meat in a stewpot.[3] Micah didn't have a camcorder; he had to paint his picture in words only; hence his savage, graphic, blistering barrage to expose the truth about these judicial officials.

Here is a corruption of vocation; these fellows are anything but civil 'servants'. They are not there to serve, but to be 'on the take'. They are not protecting rights, but crushing people. We meet the same corruption of vocation today, whether it seems low-key or severe. The Associated Press reported that, on the basis of a random audit covering a six-month period, it was estimated that over 8,000 employees of the U. S. Department of Agriculture used government credit cards for a total of $5.8 million in purchases other than for bona fide travel expenses. Or how often do we read of Christian girls in, for example, Egypt being abducted, perhaps raped, and forced into marriage to a Muslim man — yet neither the police or the authorities will lift a finger to intervene or to punish the perpetrators?

3:4
Then they will cry out to Yahweh,
and he will not answer them;
and may he hide his face from them at that time,
because of the evil they have done.

'Then', paralleled by **'at that time'** in the second half of this verse, refers to the time of punishment these officials will face — that is, the disasters Micah has already predicted in chapters 1 – 2. These vultures will then **'cry out to Yahweh'**. They may be crooks, but they are always in church for the day of national fasting and prayer. Micah says they will **'cry out'** to Yahweh. This verb ($z\bar{a}\,{}^{\prime}aq$) connotes a cry for help in distress but does not by itself imply repentance.[4] And, as Allen points out, the verb carries with it a certain irony:

> The term *cry out* is a technical one for appeal to a judge for help against victimization. The woman of Shunem exercised this legal right of protest when she returned home after seven years in Philistia and found her farm taken over by others: she appealed to the king, who saw to it that justice was done (2 K. 8:1-6). No such equity had these judges shown. In return they

would find their own appeals to God unavailing in their hour of need.[5]

Micah promises that these predators, otherwise known as public servants, will be disappointed in religion. It will not prove the bomb-shelter they were hoping for. Calvin hits the mark:

> Thus, Micah confronts us here with *the greatest evil that could ever befall us*, that is, that God rejects those who reject him, and that God refuses to answer them, so that all their prayers are in vain and are no longer received by God.[6]

The last half of this verse can be taken either in an indicative sense ('and he will hide his face from them') or as a subjunctive (**'may he hide...'**).[7] Either way the overall thrust is not changed.

3:5
Here's what Yahweh says about the prophets,
who are leading my people astray;
when they are munching on something they preach peace,
but when someone will not give what they demand,
    they consecrate war against him.

Now Micah announces Yahweh's word 'concerning' or 'against' (the preposition can have either meaning) the prophets. Sadly, Yahweh says they **'are leading my people astray'**. It is not the need of the people but the greed of the prophet that drives them. Literally, the third line reads, 'When they bite with their teeth, they preach peace.' The verb 'bite' (*nāšak*) elsewhere always (ten times) refers to a snake's bite (cf. Num. 21:6,8,9; Eccles. 10:11; Amos 5:19). Perhaps there is an innuendo here implying that these prophets' bite is as lethal as a serpent's. The idea is that, as long as the prophets are feeding on the 'perks' people give them,

they promise those folk prosperity and success
(**'peace'**). But those who don't hand over the goodies
receive a drastic and threatening message: **'they
consecrate war against him'**. The way these 'losing'
listeners are described is a bit tricky. Literally, the text
reads, 'whoever will not give at / upon their mouth'.
Some (e.g., ESV, NASB) take this as to 'put nothing
into their mouths'; however 'upon their mouth' elsewhere seems to refer to speech and, used with 'give',
means to pay up what is demanded.[8] So, those who
don't pay the higher clergy fees these prophets ask for,
or who can't give a generous gift to their 'ministry',
inevitably catch the prophets' ire.

There is nothing wrong with a prophet receiving a
'clergy fee'. As Achtemeier points out, it was customary
for prophets in Israel to be given gifts or fees in return
for services (1 Sam. 9:7-8; 1 Kings 14:3; 2 Kings 4:42;
8:7-9). The sin of Micah's opponents, however, is that
'they are letting the size of the fee determine the content of their prophecy'.[9] If you were to butter them up
and stump up the shekels from your money-market
account, there was a 'prosperity gospel' for you. The
prophet's eyes would light up and he would exclaim,
'Something *good* is going to happen to you!'

3:6-7
Therefore, you will have night with no vision,
and you will have darkness with no divination —
the sun shall go down upon the prophets,
and the day become dark over them.
And the seers shall be disgraced,
and the diviners ashamed —
all of them shall cover their mouths,
for there is no answer from God.

But something good will not happen to these prophets. With that ominous **'therefore'**, Micah announces
the judgement for this perversion of the prophetic

office. The judgement does not consist in blazing fire or foreign invasion, but in silence and darkness.

Micah means that these prophets will no longer receive any word from God: **'You will have night with no vision'**, or, 'You will have night instead of vision' (again, the preposition can be taken as 'without' or as 'in place of'). A vision was one of the vehicles through which Yahweh would communicate his word to prophets (Isa. 1:1; cf. Num. 12:6-8). But instead of that these prophets would have **'night'**. Yahweh will take away his word from these impostors. Hence **'the sun shall go down'** on them and the **'day become dark'** over them (3:6). They would have no light from God's word, no access to it. They may want it, but there will be **'no answer from God'** (3:7), just as he will not answer the butcher-leaders who try prayer in their emergency (3:4).

What, however, are we to make of Micah's allusion to diviners and divination here? Divination was strictly forbidden for Israel (Deut. 18:9-14), but was practised nevertheless (2 Kings 17:14-18). Pagan diviners might look for omens in the way arrows fell to the ground, or in the configuration of an animal's liver (cf. Ezek. 21:21), and on this basis offer guidance.[10] But Micah's purpose here is not to discuss legitimate and illegitimate means of receiving divine revelation. His broadside simply underscores that, regardless of the techniques they may employ, God will give no word to these men. Why should we be surprised if some of Judah's prophets were practitioners of the paranormal? No matter, he says; whatever they try won't work. Yahweh is withdrawing his word (cf. Amos 8:11-12) — he will impart no more revelation to these prophets.

We might pause to ponder this. Some might say that God can't withdraw his word today thanks to Gutenberg; after all, we have Scripture, the Word of God, in writing — and fifty-eight kinds of study Bibles available from evangelical publishers. But God can still 'take away' his word. He may take away the desire for it or interest in it. Who can doubt that this judgement may well be upon the church, the evangelical church, in the West? Our people know more about Britney Spears than the book of Ezekiel. In my part of the USA most professing Christian men know more about Southeastern Conference football than they do about the Psalms. We abuse — and then lose — the Word of God.

3:8
Yet I, I have been filled with power,
    that is, with the Spirit of Yahweh —
    and with justice and might
to declare to Jacob his rebellion
and to Israel his sin.

Graciously, God has left a faithful witness in Judah. With a strong adversative and an emphatic pronoun, **'Yet I, I ...'**, Micah contrasts his own ministry with that of the 'mainline' prophets of verses 5-7. Hence he implies that there is a degree of loneliness about his ministry as he swims against the stream of current prophetic trends (3:5-7). Like Jesus, however, Micah can say, 'Yet I am not alone' (John 16:32). For in his isolation he is equipped with a certain energy for his task: **'I have been filled with power.'** Yahweh has fortified him for his work. There is some question about how to take the phrase **'the Spirit of Yahweh'** prefaced with the particle *'et*. The particle can be construed as a preposition, 'with the help of', and so may indicate the Spirit as the agent of the power (see NJPS); or it may be an accusative marker to be taken as 'that is' or 'namely'.[11] Hence the Spirit of Yahweh is identified as the 'power' with which Micah is filled.
    Although the prophet probably intends **'power'**, **'justice'** and **'might'** to be understood together as a

verbal collage depicting Yahweh's enabling, each term hits a distinctive note. **'Power'** (*kōaḥ*) means 'physical and psychic strength to stand up against opposition and discouragement'.[12] Yahweh, as the everlasting God, 'keeps on giving power to the faint' (Isa. 40:29). In contrast to magistrates who 'despise' justice (3:9) and don't give a toss about it (3:1), Micah is filled with **'justice'** (*mišpāṭ*); he refers to his commitment to the standards of Yahweh's covenant and to his passion for his 'right order' to prevail.[13] This, incidentally, reminds us that character, and not merely gifts (cf. 'power'), stamps a servant as genuine. He does not simply 'make a living', but there is a certain godly passion that percolates within him and drives his ministry. And then Micah is filled with **'might'**, *gĕbûrâ*, with manliness or courage ('guts', as we say), 'which does not ... weakly adapt itself to the judgement of the many and great, but stands up boldly for divine right and truth'.[14]

Finally, Micah specifies his task: **'to declare to Jacob his rebellion and to Israel his sin'**. His is largely a negative ministry; he focuses on the criticizing function of the word of God. Chapters 1-3 show Micah at work in this way. There will always be something surgical about faithful preaching; it will always seek to expose undetected rebellion and hidden idolatry. Genuine believers realize how healthy this is and rejoice to have their sin exposed in this way.

In one verse the prophet has encapsulated his ministry: his loneliness (3:8a), his equipment (3:8b) and his task (3:8c). A ministry like his, it seems, is the only antidote to the perversion of preaching in the land.

3:9-11a
Now hear this,
leaders of the house of Jacob and rulers of the house of
　　　Israel,

who despise justice
and make crooked all that's straight,
building Zion with bloodshed
and Jerusalem with wrong;
her leaders judge for a bribe,
her priests teach for a price,
and her prophets divine for money...

In verses 9-12 Micah highlights the crimes (3:9-11a),
the theology (3:11b) and the end (3:12) of Judah's
leaders. His **'Now hear'** in the opening line of verse 9
picks up the same note from verse 1. He once more
(see 3:1) addresses Judah's magistrates (3:9) without
ignoring her clergy (3:11).

With typical prophetic skill, Micah accuses as he
describes. He epitomizes the leaders' *attitude* (they
'despise justice'), which in turn drives their *actions*
(they **'make crooked all that's straight'**; cf. Isa. 5:20)
— they have the knack of perverting all that is proper
and legal to their own ends. In verse 10 he exposes
their *method*: **'building Zion with bloodshed and
Jerusalem with wrong'**.[15] 'Bloodshed' is *dāmîm*, the
plural form, which indicates the shedding of blood
through violence.[16]

Who knows precisely how the blood was shed and
the wrong done? We have evidence that Jerusalem's
population mushroomed in the latter half of the eighth
century BC; it grew from a site of thirty-seven acres to
one of 150 acres. It's likely that much of this influx
came from residents of the northern kingdom seeking
refuge from the Assyrian incursions of Tiglath-pileser
III, Shalmaneser V and Sargon II.[17] What a splendid
'opportunity' for those in public office at that very
time! Perhaps the bloodshed came from mercilessly
driving something like forced labour gangs in con-
structing urban expansion projects. Or perhaps the
bloodshed came from the Mafia-like 'disappearance' of

people who stood in the way of progress and profits. These fellows knew how to play it rough.[18]
Then Micah mocks their *passion*. The words, **'bribe'**, **'price'** and **'money'** (literally, 'silver') say it all. Magistrate, priest and prophet are all holding their hands out.[19] Allen summarizes 'the services available in the capital' as follows:

> A legal problem? Take it to the judge. A religious problem? Take it to the priest. A personal problem? Take it to the prophet. A satisfactory answer was guaranteed if money passed from hand to hand.[20]

What a strange deity Micah serves! J. J. Finkelstein says that in the Mesopotamian texts there is no known cuneiform law specifically outlawing bribery; in fact, it was 'not only a common practice, but was recognized as a legal transaction'.[21] In paganism bribery and 'fees' would pad out your retirement account; in Judah they would bring you divine judgement.

3:11b
… yet they lean upon Yahweh, saying,
  'Isn't Yahweh among us?
  Disaster will never come upon us.'

Micah now informs us of the *doctrine* that these justice-despising, law-twisting, blood-stained, money-grubbing leaders and clergy hold, the belief that gives them a secure 'faith'. He says they lean **'upon Yahweh'** (the phrase is emphatic). He is more sarcastic than serious. He means they lean upon their interpretation of Yahweh's promises. He quotes their sentiment: **'Isn't Yahweh among us? Disaster will never come upon us.'** Wherever did they get that idea? They had chapter and verse. It was the Lord's word to Solomon at the construction of the temple:

> As for this house you are building — if you walk in my statutes and will do my ordinances, and if you shall guard all my commandments to walk in them, then I shall carry out my promise with you, which I spoke to David your father, and I shall dwell in the midst of the sons of Israel, and I will never forsake my people Israel (1 Kings 6:12-13).[22]

They latched hold of verse 13 and ignored verse 12, took the promise and skipped the conditions. The promise became their rabbit's foot, a religious security blanket, a pledge of immunity. They were safe no matter what. It's not difficult to imagine this happening — one can pervert promises as well as justice.[23]

3:12
Therefore, because of you
  Zion will be turned into a ploughed field,
  Jerusalem a heap of ruins,
  and the temple mount an overgrown height.

With the opening **'therefore'** Micah declares the judgement on Judah thanks to these vicious, venal leaders. Originally, **'Zion'** was the Jebusite stronghold captured by David (2 Sam. 5:7), but often in prophetic and poetic texts it stands as a synonym of Jerusalem (cf. Ps. 149:2; Isa. 4:3; 40:9).[24] Micah's pictures create a collage of images of ruin. Zion will (literally) be 'ploughed as a field', implying that the site would be wiped clean, since 'an area had to be totally cleared of debris in order to be ploughed and planted'.[25] Jerusalem will be a **'heap of ruins'**, a monument of devastation (the singular 'heap' was used of Samaria in 1:6), and the temple mount (literally, 'the mountain of the house') **'an overgrown height'** (*bāmôt yā'ar*). This last suggests a place abandoned for so long that it has reforested itself. And Micah may be adding a special dig in referring to the temple mount as *bāmôt* (literally, 'high places'). He equated Jerusalem with these paganized shrines in 1:5; by using the same word in reference to the temple mount he may imply that the worship occurring there equates with the deviant devotions conducted at these illegitimate chapels.[26] There is the prophet's picture: Jerusalem / Zion — cleared off, piled up, left behind.

Yahweh had, of course, said it would be this way — if Israel proved unfaithful. The microphones for the temple dedication service (1 Kings 8) had scarcely been put away before Yahweh warned Solomon (1 Kings 9:1-9) that should he and / or Israel prove faithless, 'I will cast out from my presence this Temple that I have consecrated for my name' (1 Kings 9:7, JB).[27] Some 250 years later Micah announced that the time had arrived.

We cannot leave this verse (3:12), however, without noting how it was received in Micah's own time and how it saved the skin of Jeremiah a hundred years later. All this we find in Jeremiah 26. Jeremiah had prophesied, like Micah, that both temple and city would be laid in ruins (Jer. 26:9). The clergy establishment considered such preaching both irreligious and unpatriotic (Jer. 26:9-11) and were salivating for Jeremiah's execution. But the elders pressed an argument that apparently turned the tide: a hundred years earlier Micah of Moresheth had preached the same message (they quote Micah 3:12); King Hezekiah and his officials didn't execute him; in fact, Hezekiah responded in fear and trembling and Yahweh postponed the threatened disaster (Jer. 26:18-19). At least in Micah's day the word worked repentance and the disaster was delayed — something we might not have known had Jeremiah not stirred up that brouhaha in the temple!

Application

According to Micah, Judah is on the slippery downhill slide to disaster. In a mere twelve verses he sketches her pell-mell, mad dash to ruin. In so doing he isolates and addresses the problem areas in the nation's life that are leading her to such havoc.

First, he attacks *politics* (3:1-4) and corrupt civil officials. Micah simply assumes that politics and politicians are subject to the Word of God. Western secularists may tout their sacred cow of 'separation of church and state', but that mantra will not win them immunity from the scrutiny and judgement of God's word. Micah's attitude is akin to that of Robert Bruce (d. 1631), who, when James VI rudely and repeatedly talked with his cohorts during the sermon, cut him down to size with: 'The Lion of the tribe of Judah is now roaring in the voice of His Gospel, and it becomes all the petty kings of the earth to be silent.'

Next, Micah attacks *preaching* and preachers (3:5-8), especially the suave, perk-loving comforters of Judah. By contrast, Micah claims he is Spirit-empowered 'to declare to Jacob his rebellion and to Israel his sin' (3:8). That still is, I would hold, a proper task in a preaching ministry among God's professing people. After sitting for so long under one's preaching, many of our hearers should have to say, 'I am a far worse sinner than I ever thought I was' (not because we rant and rave and castigate, but simply because we shine the Word of God on the nooks and crannies of their habits, thoughts and imaginations). It was *after* the first year of our marriage that I began to realize how terribly selfish I was / am. So it is with many Christians; they should find that it is after they have been converted and are among the people of God that they see they are far more deeply corrupted, perverse and idolatrous than they ever imagined. Proper Micah-like preaching should do this.

Third, Micah attacks *presumption* (3:9-12). In spite of civil injustice and religious chicanery, leaders in Judah were cocksure that they would not face disaster: 'There's the temple, the place of Yahweh's presence; he would never allow...' Beware of attitudes that begin with, 'Oh, God would never...' I cannot speak for others; I can only say that there often seems to be an undertow of this presumption in my own country (USA) and it can easily filter into the minds of Christians. We may think our nation has some sort of manifest destiny — that, though America may sometimes be bungling and stupid, she is nevertheless invincible. 'Surely,' we might infer, 'God knows how many thousands of dollars for international missions come from this nation, and how many evangelical agencies and colleges and seminaries there are here, and how much support for worldwide relief work flows from this country. Surely, God would never...'[28] What would happen to the kingdom of God if he wiped such a 'support system' off the map in judgement? Nothing. God's kingdom would still come. He doesn't need arrogant 'superpowers' to help him, nor a dozen evangelical 'empires' to assist him. Some of us must keep our eye on that line between patriotism and idolatry.

The stubborn future
(Micah 4:1-5)

Let's say there is a gentleman in his mid-seventies. He has a son, now in his early fifties, who is an utter wastrel — he left his wife and two children some years ago, cannot hold down a job and boozes himself silly with what money he does get. So the older gentleman pays his lawyer a visit and recasts his will, cutting his son completely out of it and leaving his estate to his two grandchildren, who happen to be responsible young adults. The inheritance *is* passed on, but the son who showed himself unfit receives none of it. That is something like what is happening at the end of Micah 3 and the beginning of Micah 4.

But some biblical critics don't get the point. They say the opening verses of chapter 4 cannot be from Micah because they are 'clearly a direct contradiction of 3:12' (Mays). So, we are told, this passage, along with most of chapters 4 – 5, consists of various prophetic sayings added to Micah's dire prediction because some people thought Micah's horrid picture of Zion in 3:12 might not be God's last word for Judah. So Micah 4 comes from the post-exilic period, most likely after the temple was rebuilt in 516 BC.[29] Some scholars have a mental block about prophets. If a prophet has preached judgement, they are sure he would never preach hope. If hope appears in his prophecy, it has then to come from some later, not-so-gloomy prophet. In their view a prophet cannot be at all sophisticated; rather he must be a simpleton, who, if he has chosen to beat the drum of judgement, will always and only beat that drum.

It's not as simple as that, however. What many fail to note is that in these verses Micah is preaching both hope *and* judgement. To be sure, 4:1-4 is a prophecy of hope — but at the same time it is a proclamation of judgement. Micah is perfectly aware that 4:1 seems to fly in the face of 3:12. But he has slipped in a crucial phrase: **'at the end of the days'** (4:1). Now whatever that means, it refers to some time in the future, down the timeline of history, *some distance from the present situation.* And that's why 4:1-4 is a message of *judgement* to Micah's own generation! It's as though Micah says to his contemporaries, 'Now here is a picture of the coming glory of Zion and Jerusalem; but this will be "at the end of the days" — that is, it is for the future, beyond your time; you will not see it or enjoy it, for it is something removed from you; you have "neither part nor lot in this matter" [cf. Acts 8:21], for you have forfeited your place in it.' Micah proclaims the 'glory word' about Zion but, by placing it 'at the end of the days', he removes that glory from the present, disobedient generation, who will receive only the 'gory word' of 3:12. The prophets' proclamation of future hope can function as an announcement of judgement on a present, unbelieving generation. Here, Micah proclaims the coming glory — that is hope; and he also tells his contemporaries they have no place in it — that is judgement. In terms of the opening analogy, the will comes about, but the wastrel son gets none of it.

4:1
And it shall be at the end of the days
[that] the mountain of Yahweh's house
     will be established as the highest of the mountains,
and it shall be lifted up above [the] hills
and peoples shall flow up to it.

'And' is not a needless conjunction; Micah wants the reader / hearer to look at what follows in the light of the preceding verses.[30] **'At the end of the days'** here refers to a far-distant future, for it points to a time beyond the still-to-come ruin of 3:12 and to a complete reversal of it. Since the contents of verses 1-3 depict the lasting conditions of Yahweh's reign, the phrase here has a last-things ring to it.[31] Micah assures us of the *stability* of the temple mount: it will be **'established'** (*nākôn*) — that is, it will never again be pounded into the wreck and ruin of 3:12. Then he depicts its *supremacy*: it will be established **'as the highest of the mountains, and ... shall be lifted up above [the] hills'**. Micah's new geology is a put-down of pagan religion. Pagan deities allegedly dwelt on their various divine mountains; Micah chalks that up as nonsense and says Yahweh's mountain will outdo the lot of them.[32] Finally, he depicts its *attraction*: **'peoples shall flow up to it'**. As Motyer says, 'The natural impossibility of a *stream* flowing upwards is intentional. A supernatural magnetism is at work.'[33] This looks like John 6:44 on a grand scale.

4:2
And many nations shall come and say:
'Come, and let us go up to the mountain of Yahweh,
    even to the house of the God of Jacob,
and let him teach us his ways,
and let us walk in his paths'
— for Torah will go forth from Zion
    and the word of Yahweh from Jerusalem.

'Many nations shall come' — these are not Israelites, but those from the great unwashed masses; they are 'strangers to the covenants of the promise, having no hope and without God in the world' (Eph. 2:12). They will come. Micah quotes *the words of the nations* which give evidence of their conversion to Yahweh.

'**Come, and let us go up to the mountain of Yahweh, even to the house of the God of Jacob**': there
is a focused commitment; they are seeking Israel's
covenant God; they are not blabbering about feeling at
one with the universe, or developing a novel form of
spirituality by discovering 'the child within'. '**And let
him teach us his ways**': there is an intense appetite,
a teachable spirit. '**Let us walk in his paths**': there is
a transformed lifestyle; what comes in by the ears
finds its way to the feet.[34] Micah predicts large-scale
conversion among the nations and people-groups —
something that should thrill us no end. We should feel
like Alexander Bilsland at the Cambuslang communion in 1743. He was overcome while considering
Isaiah 54:5. 'What made me rejoice most of all at that
time,' he explained, 'was the last part of that text, "the
God of the whole Earth shall he be called", by which I
got a large view of the Extent of the Redeemer's Kingdom to become universal over the Whole Earth: which
prospect was most agreeable and delightful to Me.'[35]
The prophet wants you to get a large view of the
Redeemer's kingdom and to delight in it.

The last line gives *the explanation of the prophet* for
these international conversions: '**for** [NIV madden-
ingly omits this causal particle] **Torah will go forth
from Zion and the word of Yahweh from Jerusalem**'. The words '**from Zion**' are emphatic in the
Hebrew text. It's not from Tyre or Nineveh, or any
enlightenment-centre of choice. Only from the former
heap of ruins (3:12) does the life-changing revelation
come. So the Bible continues on its offensive way with
its exclusive claims: here, and nowhere else, will you
receive the truth you need.

What about the fulfilment of verse 2? I would
suggest it is both incremental and final. One can see
foretastes of it, for example, when the Greeks come
seeking Jesus in John 12:20-26 and when the Gentile
mission takes off in Acts 10 – 11. One could argue for

an ongoing fulfilment in the fruit of Christian missions throughout the years. However, it seems to me that there is a clear 'not yet' element in the fulfilment (especially when verses 3-4 are kept in view). We haven't yet seen anything like this or Zechariah 8:20-23 in final, definitive form.[36]

4:3
And he shall judge between many peoples,
and he shall reprove strong nations a long way off;
and they shall beat their swords into ploughshares
    and their spears into pruning knives;
nation will not lift up sword against nation,
nor will they learn war any more.

In these days not only does Yahweh's word go forth, but Yahweh himself acts: **'he shall judge ... he shall reprove'**. **'Judge'** (*šāpaṭ*) here means that he 'puts things right'. This is good news. This is what Psalm 96 celebrates when it promises that Yahweh 'will judge [Heb., *dîn*] the peoples with equity' (v. 10); the psalmist then commands creation — including sea, fields and trees — to pull out all the stops in an orgy of doxology before Yahweh, 'for he comes, for he comes to judge [*šāpaṭ*] the earth' (v. 13). Yahweh's coming to judge is good news for his people because he will put things right: 'he will judge the world with righteousness, and the peoples with his truth' (v. 13). Micah implies that Yahweh will impose his justice on the nations even if they are **'strong'** ('superpowers') and control them even if they are distant (**'a long way off'**).

As a result, **'swords'** and **'spears'**, which represent the whole gamut of weaponry or war *matériel*, will be hammered into farming and gardening tools. We can't be precise about the **'ploughshares'** (*'ittîm*); the word may more properly refer to plough-points or possibly mattocks (REB).[37] In any case, farming is the wave of the future; tanks will be turned into tractors, bombs into balers and missiles into milking parlours. The last two clauses flesh out what this means: **'nation will not lift up sword against nation'** (the very reverse of what Jesus said would characterize the present age, Mark 13:8), **'nor will they learn war any more'**. Both military academies and terrorist training camps will be shut down.

We can make two observations about verse 3. One has to do with *sphere*. The scene here is earth, not heaven. Peoples and nations, swords and spears, ploughs and pruning shears are very this-worldly. The turf is earth. Interpreters may look at it differently — some will posit a 'millennial' earth; some will see the 'new' earth. But it is earth. Yahweh will put things right *here*. Micah doesn't want you floating off to heaven at this point.[38] Yahweh will impose the right order on the real estate that has always belonged to him.

The second observation is about *sequence*. The verb form here, **'they shall beat'** (*wĕkittĕtû*), is clearly the consequence of the two preceding verbs, **'he shall judge ... reprove'**.[39] In spite of what politicians with their heads in the clouds or sentimental graduation speakers imply when they quote only the last half of this verse, this universal peace does not come because nations finally turn against war in disgust, or the UN eventually got its corrupt house in order, or governments at last began reading political pronouncements issued by church hierarchies. No, 'he shall judge ... they shall beat'. *Divine intervention brings about international pacification.* People and nations do not produce this state of affairs by their own efforts, or brilliance, or exhaustion. Rather, Yahweh imposes his just rule and, because of that, nations exist in peace.

4:4
And they shall sit — each man under his vine
   and under his fig tree —

with no one terrifying [them],
for the mouth of Yahweh of hosts has spoken.

Micah goes on to describe the peace Yahweh will bring
about. We must not miss the beneficiaries of these
conditions; the **'they'** in **'they shall sit'** refers in this
context to folk from the nations and peoples of verses
2-3 — i.e., Gentiles. Micah does not exclude believing
Israelites, but they are not his concern here. Moreover, notice the stress on the individual: **'they shall
sit — *each man* under his vine and under his fig
tree'**. The scope is vast (peoples, nations, 4:3); the
benefit is particular (**'each man'**); the peace is univer-
sally prevalent but individually enjoyed. This is vin-
tage Yahweh — he does not lose sight of his people in
the crowd; he does not see huge blobs, but individual
persons.

This verse is unique to Micah. The parallel passage
in Isaiah 2:1-4 does not contain this picture. The
verse underscores the enjoyment of this peace. Israel
had enjoyed a historical approximation to these conditions under Solomon's reign (1 Kings 4:24-25), and
yet it remains a future hope for Gentile converts (here)
and restored Israel (Zech. 3:10; note the *social* element in Zechariah — everyone invites 'his neighbour'
under his vine and fig tree!).

Egyptian tomb paintings, Assyrian reliefs and
the biblical writers commonly use the phrase
[sitting under one's vine and fig tree] to refer to a
people who control their own lives, without foreign interference, and are able to cultivate the
land which the gods / God has given to them
(1 Kings 4:25; Is. 36:16). The vine and fig provided some shade as well as fruit, and enjoying
them indicated some long-term prospects as
each took several years to become productive.[40]

Micah also stresses the security and certainty of this peace. **'With no one terrifying [them]'** (traditionally, 'none shall make them afraid') assures that no one can or will destroy, interrupt, or reverse the enjoyment of this peace (see also Lev. 26:6; Jer. 30:10; 46:27; Ezek. 34:28; 39:26; Zeph. 3:13).[41] What a treasured word this must be to many of Christ's flock in North Korea, China, Indonesia, Pakistan and dozens of other places! The world is full of terror and hatred and butchering for Jesus' people. But Yahweh promises the day will come when he will say, 'I will place him in the safety for which he longs' (Ps. 12:5). And then Micah appends Yahweh's signature: **'... for the mouth of Yahweh of hosts has spoken'**. This is the only occurrence of **'Yahweh of hosts'** in Micah; it points to Yahweh as the one who has all resources, cosmic and earthly, at his disposal and can therefore bring about what he pleases.[42] He is the only one who can say with holy omnipotent defiance, 'I act and who can reverse it?' (Isa. 43:13, NASB). The causal **'for'** (*kî*) is important; it takes in all of the preceding verses from 4:1 to the first part of 4:4. Micah is no fool. He knows his prophecy of a world where Zion is restored, nations are converted and hungry for the Word and where peace is all-pervasive sounds like something from a fantasy. And maybe it will seem too incredible to scarred and suffering saints. Hence Micah adds his big 'for...' — as if to say, 'I know this may sound like too much, so you must understand that this is what *Yahweh* has decided.'[43]

4:5
To be sure, all the peoples will go on walking,
    each in the name of its god,
but we, we will walk
    in the name of Yahweh our God
    for ever and ever.

Here Micah 'applies' the revelation of verses 1-4 to his
own time. I take the opening particle, *kî*, in an emphatic sense — **'to be sure ...'**, or 'indeed ...'[44] The
prophet clearly acknowledges the current state of
affairs: in his day all the **'peoples'** were doing anything but flowing to Jerusalem, or hungering and
thirsting for the word of Yahweh (cf. 4:2-3). They will,
Micah confesses, for the present **'go on walking'** (a
durative imperfect; cf. Waltke), each in the name of
their god. Then we meet an adversative conjunction
(**'but'**) and a huge emphatic first-person plural pronoun (*'ănaḥnû*): **'but we, we will walk'**. Micah's **'we'**
does not encompass the whole nation of Judah, for
his previous denunciations show that there were
many in Judah who didn't care in the slightest for
walking **'in the name of Yahweh our God'**. Micah's
'we' embraces himself and all the believing, faithful
remnant in Judah who are determined not to ape 'all
the peoples', but to form a counter-culture to them.
Just because peoples and nations are not yet coming
and longing for Yahweh's word, as verse 2 predicts,
that is no reason why Yahweh's remnant cannot do so
now. It's as if Micah is saying, 'Verses 1-4 are down
the timeline in the future, but we believers in Judah
can begin to live that way *now*; the day will come
when many nations will say, "Let us walk in his
paths," but we will walk "in his name" today; we can
live a last-days lifestyle in these days!' Note also that
this is an 'unending commitment ("for ever and ever")
rather than a momentary foxhole cry for help while
they are in a tough spot'.[45]

Application

The core of Micah's testimony in 4:1-5 is that *nothing is going to
keep God's kingdom from coming* — and coming completely.

Hence, he highlights first *the surprise of God's kingdom* (4:1). Zion will become Dirtville (3:12), but Yahweh will raise up his kingdom out of those ruins; his kingdom does not come because conditions are favourable. I think of the way David Searle describes Barvas on the Isle of Lewis as 'one of the most desolate spots on God's earth', with its 'monotonous peat moors and bogs', its brine-soaked Atlantic winds and inhospitable climate — and yet God chose to display his glory there in the 1949 revival.[46] Desolate circumstances are no obstacle to Yahweh's power.

Secondly, Micah underscores *the passion for God's word* the nations will have (4:1-2) and indicates that Yahweh's word is the instrument behind coming international transformation ('for Torah will go forth from Zion and the word of Yahweh from Jerusalem'). If that will be the case then, should not this same word be at the centre of the church's ministry now? Is Zion despising her unique treasure in our day? Has the church traded her birthright for a mess of entertainment, kids' clubs, quilting classes and support groups for left-handers?

Third, the prophet hammers home *the impact of God's justice* (4:3-4). The idyllic sword-to-ploughshare peace does not come as the apex of human achievement, but from the imposition of divine justice. This does not mean we should not seek for rational understanding and peaceful relations among nations. But we must have a biblical realism about all such efforts. They will, at best, be partial and relative. The hope of the world rests in divine intervention, not in some dreamy human evolution.

And then Micah leads the way in charting *the path of God's remnant* (4:5). He commits himself and his fellow believers in Judah to live a 'new Zion' form of life in their current circumstances. There is the grand time promised (4:1-4) and then there are the grim times in which Micah and his contemporaries live — and he calls Yahweh's remnant to live a grand-time life in their grim-time situations. Helmut Thielicke tells of life in Stuttgart during World War II and of being in the (formerly) magnificent house of an industrialist, Mr Knoll, after an Allied bombing raid had made rubble and ashes of a good bit of it. Thielicke was rolling up his shirtsleeves to begin the clean-up when he was greeted by Mr. Knoll, 'impeccably dressed and with a flower in his buttonhole'. He

invited Thielicke to share a tiny, undamaged corner near the
kitchen, where a small coffee table was set with a dazzling white
cloth and fine china — and a single rose thriving in a vase on the
table.[47] Chaos and destruction are all around — but at least there,
in that corner, life as it ought to be goes on. That is Micah's call: to
live the life of the next age in the ruins of the present one. Who
knows what it may cost to walk through the unbelief and ridicule of
one's own generation? But we must walk on in the name of
Yahweh our God while we await 'the end of the days'.

Chewed up, spat out?
(Micah 4:6-8)

There were two problems in Micah's preaching: the marvellous future of many nations in the kingdom Yahweh brings (4:1-4) and the dismal future of Jerusalem / Judah in 3:12. If Zion / Jerusalem will be in ruins and many nations will be drawn to Yahweh, what about Judah herself? Will Jerusalem go on being ploughed like a field and standing as a heap of ruins? Are they, the original covenant people, cut off completely from this marvellous future? Do none of them have any part in it? Here Micah says no, *God holds out hope for his ruined people*.[48]

4:6
In that day, says Yahweh,
I will gather the lame
and I will assemble the outcast
— those on whom I brought disaster...

'In that day' connects verses 6-7 to what takes place in verses 1-4, 'at the end of the days'; as there is a glorious future then for the nations, so there will be for decimated Judah 'in that day'. Yahweh speaks in the first person and probably uses the language of a shepherd when he describes his people as **'lame'** and **'outcast'**; on the latter (the root is *nādaḥ*), see Ezekiel 34:4,16 (where ESV has 'strayed') and Jeremiah 23:2,3,8 (where the causative stem describes Yahweh's flock as 'driven away'). Micah then adds an *id *est* (= 'that is to say') phrase to identify precisely who these lame and outcasts are: **'those on whom I brought disaster'**. This harks back to the judgements of 3:12 and 2:1-5 and views them as having taken place.

4:7

… and I shall make the lame into a remnant
and those driven off into a strong nation,
and Yahweh shall reign over them in Mt Zion
      from now on and for ever.

Now Yahweh shows how he will transform this bunch of disaster-struck outcasts: **'I shall make the lame into a remnant.'** The verb *śîm* ('to make, put') plus the following preposition *lĕ* ('to') indicates a transformation, like that of a sea into dry land (Exod. 14:21), rivers into islands (Isa. 42:15), mountains into a road (Isa. 49:11), shame into praise and renown (Zeph. 3:19 — note the use of 'lame' and 'outcast' in that text), or a city into a ruin (1:6). The verb also governs the next line: Yahweh will make those **'driven off'**, or 'away', **'into a strong nation'** (cf. the 'strong nations' Yahweh will reprove in 4:3). In verse 7 Micah repeats **'lame'** from verse 6 but does not repeat 'outcast'; instead he uses a word (*nahălā'â*) which only occurs here but seems related to an adverb meaning 'way off / out'.[49] It probably refers to those who were 'sent off' or 'driven away'.

This **'remnant'**, however, does not refer to a few stragglers who somehow hang on past the last gasp. This 'remnant', as the parallel says, is also to be 'a strong nation'. Hence it will not only survive but thrive. And yet this group of people does not automatically constitute a remnant. It's likely that, when Yahweh says he will **'make the lame into'** a remnant, the verb is intended to carry some punch. The remnant is the fruit of Yahweh's restoring and preserving grace; it is not a monument to Judah's durability or to her skills in coping with her circumstances.[50]

The grammar changes in the last line — we move from a word spoken *by* Yahweh (4:6-7a) to one spoken *about* Yahweh (4:7b), from first person to third person: **'And Yahweh shall reign over them'** — i.e., over the remnant of restored lame and outcasts, **'in** [or 'on'] **Mt Zion'** (see comments on 4:8 below), **'from now on and for ever'** (cf. Isa. 24:23). This **'now'** is still in the future for Micah; he means from the time that Yahweh does his work of transforming the remnant (4:7a).

It is all too easy, however, to miss the strong assurance amid the many details of the text. Calvin therefore rightly captures the rock-anchored consolation in Yahweh's reigning over his people **'for ever'**:

> Furthermore, Micah does not say that God will reign only for a day, or for a brief time, but for ever. For if we thought that, after helping us today, God would withdraw tomorrow, and leave us in doubt as to when he might ever help us again, what sort of consolation would that be? Even if God should help us for a season or two, but we should not know about the future, we would still gain nothing. But when God assures us that his assistance will last to the very end, indeed without end, and that in life and in death we shall feel his protection and safekeeping, what greater assurance could we want?[51]

4:8
And *you*, O tower of the flock,
   O hill, O Daughter Zion,
To *you* it will come,
yes, the former dominion shall come,
   the kingdom to Daughter Jerusalem.

This verse has the commentators scratching their heads, in that one doesn't know whether it primarily connects with what precedes or with what follows it. It makes a fine heading for the depiction of messianic peace held out in 4:9 – 5:5. On the other hand, the Zion / Jerusalem links go backwards (3:12; 4:2,7) and the initial conjunction plus pronoun (**'And you…'**) ties it to verses 6-7.

Micah addresses Zion / Jerusalem as the **'tower of the flock'**. I do not think this is a specific place name (as it seems to be in Gen. 35:21), but a figurative allusion indicating Zion's importance. Towers were sometimes erected from which shepherds could keep track of their flocks. With Waltke, I take the next term (*ōpel*, **'hill'**) as a vocative, 'Ophel', so that one meets three vocatives in the first line: 'tower of the flock', 'Ophel', 'Daughter Zion'.[52] 'The Ophel' was the section of the south-east ridge of ancient Jerusalem, south of the temple platform and north of the city of David.[53] Micah may have intended this section specifically, or perhaps was simply using Ophel / hill as a synonym for Zion / Jerusalem.

After this triple address the prophet picks up the initial pronoun from the first line of the verse ('and you') and repeats it emphatically in **'to *you* it will come'**. What will come? **'Yes, the former dominion shall come.'**[54] This former dominion is likely to be the kingdom in its previous form and glory like that in the time of David. This is the kingdom that will come to **'Daughter Jerusalem'**. The 'kingdom' here is no different from that in the latter part of verse 7.

Verses 6-8 are a needed word. If Zion / Jerusalem will be rubble (3:12) and if converted nations will enjoy a glorious future centred on Zion (4:1-4), does that mean Yahweh's original covenant people are shut out of that future? Answer: 'No, Yahweh will raise up a remnant who will have their place under that regime.' But how would anyone in Micah's day know whether he/she was a part of that remnant? That person would be found at Micah's side (4:5), living a last-days lifestyle in the setting of 735 BC.

Application

Nobody these days cares much about Edsels except maybe Leroy Walker of Beulah, North Dakota. Edsels were a phenomenon of the American automobile world in the late 1950s, when some 110,000 of them were produced. These somewhat weird-looking machines proved to be one of Ford's failures. No one bothers about them or cares about them except a few die-hards who have a love affair with Edsels — like Leroy Walker, who has 226 of them scattered about his junk yard. They are extinct specimens in the automotive landfill of transportation history.

And it's easy to think of Israel as the disappointing flop in God's redemptive production plan. She has riddled her history with inconsistency, infidelity and apostasy. It would be easy to assume that God has consigned her to the oblivion and shame and scourging she so richly deserved. There she can rust and rot away far from the kingdom and glory. But Micah puts the brakes on such thinking. Yahweh is the God, he says, who will make the lame into a remnant. His teaching is the same as that in Isaiah 10:20-23 — and that of Paul in Romans 11:1-5 for that matter. Paul assures us that long before Micah's day God had been doing his remnant-collecting work. Because of the election of grace God will always have a believing Israel, however small it may seem.

But why should we — many of us formerly unwashed Gentiles who have begun to enjoy the worship and privileges of the Zion kingdom (4:1-2) — why should we really care if God keeps a faithful Israel? Because it shows us that Yahweh does not have a 'disposable' people, as if Israel was too tough a project for Yahweh to handle and he simply abandoned them like so many Edsels in a vehicular graveyard. If he does that, we are all in deep trouble. Walk your way through the textual sieve of Ephesians 2 – 3, where we understand that the people of God today constitute a single new humanity in a Jewish-Gentile church. And then ask yourself the question: 'What hope is there for the church if God simply washes his hands of his unfaithful people?' Have you checked the church's record lately? It's not exactly fantastic. So no Gentile arrogance, please. Where would any of us be without the remnant-gathering, remnant-preserving God of Israel?

The places Yahweh visits
(Micah 4:9-10)

Before jumping into the details of these verses, we must step back and see the structural map of 4:9 – 5:5a. This chunk of text consists of three segments (4:9-10; 4:11-13; 5:1-5a); each of them begins with **'Now'** (Heb., *'attâ*), or 'and now', and depicts a judgement situation; then each segment comes to an emphatic turning-point and preaches the grace that will come in, or out of, the given judgement situation.[55] Graphically, it looks like this:

4:9-10
'Now...'   Judgement (4:9-10b)
'there...'   Grace (4:10c)

4:11-13
'And now...'   Judgement (4:11)
'But *they*...'   Grace (4:12-13)

5:1-5a
'Now...'   Judgement (5:1)
'But *you*...'   Grace (5:2-5a)

Why this particular scheme? Micah wants to be clear about what Judah would suffer, to make plain the misery through which Zion would pass, and yet to show in the face of such deep distress the 'nevertheless' of Yahweh's grace. The prophet's purpose, then, is to encourage remnant-believers in Judah (cf. 4:5) to

keep clinging to the kingdom-promise even when that
kingdom is obscured as they suffer exile with all the
people. How can those of remnant faith endure in such
dark times unless they know that their labour is not in
vain, because Yahweh has salvation waiting on the
other side of the darkness?

4:9
Now … why do you cry out?
Is there no king in you?
Or has your counsellor perished,
     that anguish has seized you like a woman in labour?

Micah begins this section with **'Now'**; this 'now' does
not mean 'right now' (i.e., at the present time) but
refers to a future 'now' which he depicts. He picks up
this 'now' in verse 10 when he says, 'for now you will
go forth from the city', referring to the exile to Babylon, which is still in the future. It's as though Micah
says, 'Here is a future situation [4:9-10b] which I am
describing as already present ['now'], and then I will
show what happens in and beyond that situation
[4:10c].'[56]
     'Why do you cry out?' The verb is *rw'*, which here
indicates a shout of alarm.[57] It is the second feminine
singular form because Micah still addresses Judah as
Daughter Zion / Jerusalem (see 4:8). At the end of the
verse the prophet compares this alarm to the anguish
that dominates a woman in labour.
     Why all the alarm and anguish? That's what Micah
wants to know. After all, he asks, **'Is there no king in
you? Or has your counsellor perished?'** Scholars
disagree over what Micah's question means. Is the
king/counsellor God, or a reigning, human Davidic
king? I think he means a human king.[58] His command
to 'writhe and scream' in verse 10 fits better with an
inadequate human king. And what of the *tone* of the
question? With Mackay I think it breathes sarcasm.

It's as though the prophet said, 'Why all this rumpus and terror? Isn't your king and counsellor [or, 'your king and his counsellors'] among you? Isn't the government still in place? So why are you bouncing off the walls like a woman in labour?' The answer is partly because the king is of no use to help or deliver. As Allen says, 'Micah satirizes the failure of human leadership.'

4:10
Writhe and scream, Daughter Zion,
    like a woman in labour;
for now you will go forth from the city,
and you shall dwell in open country,
and you shall go to Babylon;
    there you will be delivered;
    there Yahweh will redeem you from the grip of your
        enemies.

Now the prophet confirms that Daughter Zion's cry is precisely the proper response and so commands her to **'writhe and scream'** like a woman in labour. **'Scream'** is a bit of a guess. The verb (*gyh*) in its five or six usages seems to mean something like 'burst forth'.[59] I am taking it as what 'bursts forth' in speech from a woman in the anguish of childbirth. The reason for such dire agony is that she (Zion, standing for Judah's population) will **'go forth from the city'** (probably Jerusalem) and end up in Babylon — in exile. Zion is homeless. It is here, however, that Micah springs his surprise. No sooner does he mention **'Babylon'** than he appends two clauses, each beginning with an emphatic **'there'** (*sam*). Babylon is the bad news, but it is precisely there that deliverance will begin. Who would ever have thought that Babylon and redemption could be mentioned in the same breath? **'There Yahweh will redeem you.'**[60]

It is well to note that this 'prophecy of exile in Babylon ... could have been known to Micah only by divine inspiration, particularly since Assyria was the dominant power at that time'.[61] Many biblical scholars would dispute that statement. They would say that we would never see a word about exile in Babylon until the neo-Babylonian empire appeared on the historical scene.[62] For them one can't have a prophecy, a 'prediction', about Babylon before Babylon, as it were. But you must understand *why* they say that. They are not led to that position by grammatical or historical arguments, but largely by philosophical preference. Imagine a father who lays it down that squash casserole is never to be served in his household. Is this because squash is poisonous, or because it has been proved to be utterly non-nutritious? No. It's because he himself does not like squash. It's because of a *bias* he has. So too, many biblical scholars will not have predictive prophecy because they do not like or want predictive prophecy. If you find Micah speaking of Babylon 130 years before Babylon really hit the morning newspapers, then one must be dealing with a 'God in heaven who reveals mysteries' (Dan. 2:28). Many biblical critics do not want to do that; they do their work 'without a God-hypothesis', as they say. Biblical critics have had a long-standing allergy to supernaturalism. When they pooh-pooh predictive prophecy they are not operating from arguments but from appetite.

Application

Micah's message here unfolds in three steps: first, anguish depicted (4:9-10a); secondly, anguish explained (i.e., 'you will go to Babylon', 4:10b); and, thirdly, anguish transformed ('there ... there ...', 4:10c). So the place of judgement becomes the beginning point of deliverance. Babylon represents the stroke of God's anger and yet is the first step of his restoration. We should never be surprised at the places where Yahweh begins his recovery work.

During the years of the revival on the Isle of Lewis there was, according to Kenneth MacDonald, a Free Church elder in Garrabost, on the Point, who was completely opposed to the revival. He really had prayed for revival, but of course it could not come through the Church of Scotland![63] Yet much of it did. What does one do when revival comes in the 'wrong' place?

And what does one do when deliverance begins in what is apparently the wrong place? Welcome it and rejoice. This word isn't only for people in Judah. Even among commentary readers there may be some of you who know that you have blatantly hardened your heart against God's ways and the Spirit's pleas, who have blocked your ears so you wouldn't hear Christ's commands; you rationalized your disobedience so you could go your own way. And God has allowed your rebellion to bear its bitter fruit. He has — in a sense — brought you to Babylon. And now what? It may be that, like the prodigal in the far country, he has brought you to the end of yourself. Well, you can repent in 'Babylon'. You can say in this bleak and homeless and strange and unwelcome place, 'I am going to submit to Yahweh's rule; I am going to ask him to make me his servant again, and I will live under the sway of Jesus whether he changes my circumstances or not.' God has a knack for beginning deliverance in Babylon.

Surprise!
(Micah 4:11-13)

'And now' (like 'now' in 4:9) introduces a disastrous future situation (4:11) as though it were already present, while verses 12-13 disclose its reversal. The text moves from the rhetoric of nations (4:11) to the secret of Yahweh (4:12) to the triumph of Zion (4:13).

4:11
And now …
many nations gather themselves against you;
they keep saying,
   'Let her be defiled,
   and let our eyes gaze upon Zion!'

The prophet addresses Zion (**'you'**) as the object of the plot hatched by the gathered nations and puts words into their mouths which indicate their intent. They want Zion to be 'defiled' (*ḥānap*). The root idea of the verb seems to indicate something twisted or perverted; it sometimes refers to polluting the land (or earth) by bloodshed (Num. 35:33; Ps. 106:38) and / or misdeeds (Isa. 24:5; Jer. 3:2,9). But the next verb shows clearly what they have in mind: **'Let our eyes gaze upon Zion!'** This means 'gaze' in the sense of 'gloat' over Zion's utter ruin. Achtemeier holds that there is a sexual nuance intended, since the prophets depict the humiliation and defeat of a people in terms of a woman stripped naked before her lovers or captors (see Nahum 3:5; Isa. 47:3; Lam. 1:8; Ezek. 16:37).[64]

The nations intend to feast their eyes on the woman they have 'finished off' and ruined.

What then does Micah mean to depict here? I agree with Keil that these verses refer to those events predicted in Joel 3, Ezekiel 38 – 39 and Zechariah 12; 14 — 'to the last great attack which the nations of the world will make upon the church of the Lord, that has been redeemed from Babel and sanctified, with the design of exterminating the holy city of God from the face of the earth'.[65] That is, we are dealing here with a last-things scenario, or, to use the buzzword, this is 'eschatological'. This, it seems to me, is the most cogent view in the context of Micah 4. We have met **'many nations'** before verse 11 — in verse 2, in what would be called an 'eschatological' setting. In verse 2 many nations throng to join Yahweh's people; here many nations gather to crush Yahweh's people. You have both strands of truth in the witness of biblical prophecy: many nations will want to receive Yahweh's word, and many nations will want to liquidate Yahweh's people. And Micah puts it all within one chapter.

4:12
But *they* do not know the plans of Yahweh
and they do not understand his decision,
for he has gathered them like cut grain
    to the threshing-floor.

In verse 11 Micah depicts the nations' assault; here he discloses their ignorance. The opening pronoun is emphatic: **'But *they* do not know.'** They have missed a huge piece of intelligence. They have no clue about the **'plans of Yahweh'**, nor do they have any notion about his **'decision'** (literally, 'his counsel') in this scenario. The prophet lets us in on Yahweh's secret: **'for he has gathered them like cut grain to the threshing-floor'**. They think they have gathered to destroy, but Yahweh has gathered them for destruction. They are only Yahweh's lackeys, carrying out *his* plan. This is the bad news in predestination that Yahweh has periodically to press upon cocky nations and arrogant rulers who swagger their way through history:

> Have you not heard
>   that I determined it long ago?
> I planned from days of old
>   what now I bring to pass,
> that you should turn fortified cities
>   into heaps of ruins...
>   (2 Kings 19:25, ESV).

Then (as with Assyria) he tells the rest of his plan:

> I will put my hook in your nose
>   and my bit in your mouth,
> and I will turn you back on the way
>   by which you came
>   (2 Kings 19:28, ESV).

4:13
Rise and thresh, Daughter Zion!
— for I will make your horn iron
and I will make your hooves bronze,
and you shall pulverize many peoples
— and devote their unjust gain to Yahweh,
    their wealth to the Lord of all the earth.

This time, however, the nations don't get off that easily. It's likely the prophet is quoting Yahweh when he orders Zion to **'rise and thresh'**. If the nations thought they were going to pillage the grain at the threshing-floor, they find out — too late — that they themselves are the grain and that Zion has become a 'super-heifer' to trample them down![66] Yahweh promises to make Zion's **'horn iron'** and her **'hooves bronze'**; she will gore with her horn (cf. Deut. 33:17;

1 Kings 22:11) and trample with her hooves.[67] The next line, **'you shall pulverize many peoples'**, fits especially with Zion's hoof-work at the threshing-floor. Hopeless Zion (4:11) has become invincible Zion. Some dispute centres on the last verb in the verse. As it stands it is a first-person singular ('I shall devote'), with Yahweh understood as the subject; or the verb may have an archaic second-person singular ending, in which case Zion would be the understood subject ('you shall devote'). The verb itself is *ḥāram*, 'to devote to destruction', 'to put under the ban' (remember Jericho, Josh. 6:18,21). To *ḥāram* 'involves the exclusion of an object from the use or abuse of humanity and its irrevocable surrender to God. Surrendering something to God meant devoting it to the service of God or putting it under utter destruction.'[68] Here Zion will devote (i.e., will put off limits and confine to Yahweh's use) the **'unjust gain'** and the **'wealth'** of the nations to **'the Lord of all the earth'** (a title first used of Yahweh in Joshua 3:11,13). It will be quite a beating at the threshing-floor: the nations will be both crushed and impoverished.

Application

William Shirer writes of early December 1941 when a lead battalion of a German infantry division had reached a suburb of Moscow and could see through field glasses the spires of the Kremlin. What the Germans didn't know, however, would hurt them. Despite huge early losses, the Russians 'had amassed in great secrecy before their capital a force more formidable than the Germans could possibly imagine' — seven armies, two cavalry tank corps, in all one hundred divisions of fresh troops equipped for fighting in terrible cold and deep snow. On 6 December 1941, this massive horde hit the Germans on a two-hundred-mile front outside Moscow and drove them back with heavy losses.[69] This doomed Germany's hope of knocking the Soviets out of the war. But they did not know...

That is a tiny analogue of what Micah pictures. The time will come when the muscles and masses of the nations will stand arrayed and salivating over the people of God. 'But they do not know the plans of Yahweh.' God's people should find solid encouragement here. In fact, you may fear that the cultural and physical assaults of the nations today are going to overwhelm Messiah's people. 'But *they* do not know the plans of Yahweh.'

Of course, if you live in the West, you may say that you simply don't like this violent, warlike scenario depicted in this text. If so, you had better cash in your hand-cream version of Christianity and get back to the Bible and get Psalms 83 and 94 back into your bloodstream. You have to realize that Christ's people desperately need the bolstering in this text — that, on the day when many nations think they have Messiah's people ready for rape and ruin, Christ will fulfil his office of King by ruling and defending us and by restraining and conquering all his and our enemies.[70] That's why there is still hope for us in this violence-racked, justice-twisting, church-destroying world.

Small town on God's map
(Micah 5:1-5a)

Here we meet the third **'now'**. Three times (4:9-10; 4:11-13; 5:1-5a) Micah introduces a period of distress with his 'now' and then follows it with a proclamation of hope. The shape of our passage moves from prophetic address (5:1, Micah speaking to Zion / Jerusalem) to divine announcement (5:2, where Yahweh speaks), to parenthetical explanation (5:3, explaining how verses 1 and 2 can fit together), to expanded assurance (5:4-5a, where Micah fleshes out what the reign of the coming ruler of verse 2 will be like). We will try to deal with the tricky details without losing sight of the main thrust of the passage.

5:1
Now round up a troop, daughter of troops
— siege is laid against us;
with a rod they strike on the jaw the leader of Israel.

NIV omits the **'now'** (*'attâ*), the first Hebrew word in this verse. This obscures the overall structure of Micah's material and the parallel this verse forms with 4:9 and 4:11. Once more this 'now' section introduces a distressing situation for Judah or, in this case, probably Jerusalem in particular. Micah pictures a **'siege'** that is set **'against us'**. Note how in that **'us'** he identifies himself with his people. This does not necessarily mean that Micah actually endured the siege, but simply that, as he envisaged it taking place, he placed himself alongside his people. Literally, the text reads, 'he has laid siege,' and NKJV takes the 'he' as referring to God, whereas others assume it refers to the enemy (hence NASB, 'they have laid siege against us'); I have taken it impersonally (what 'someone' has done) and so translated it as a passive.

We can't be sure exactly what it is that Micah calls Jerusalem to do in face of the siege. His command uses a word- or sound-play; he wants the 'daughter of *gĕdûd'* to *gādad* in some way! There may be two distinct verbs that 'use' that *gādad* root. One means to 'gash'; hence NJPS, 'Now you gash yourself in grief' (cf. 1 Kings 18:28). The other means 'to throng' or 'band together'.[71] This latter fits nicely with *gĕdûd*, a band of raiders. Micah may have chosen this term to suggest Zion's meagre military resources — they could not muster an army, but only a mere detachment, the equivalent of a raiding party.[72] Hence my translation: **'Round up a troop, daughter of troops.'**

The next line implies the success of the siege: **'With a rod they strike on the jaw the leader** [literally, "judge"] **of Israel.'** It's likely that this is a reference to a reigning king and that he is completely in the hands of the enemy; they can do with him as they will. There is probably a sound-play in this line: **'rod'** is *šēbeṭ*; **'leader'** is *šōpēṭ*, or roughly anglicized, 'With a *shay-vet* they strike the *show-fate* of Israel.' It's hard to pick that up in English; maybe something like 'a beater for the leader' gets close. I don't think this was fulfilled in the Assyrian siege of Jerusalem in 701 BC. Sennacherib didn't have Hezekiah in his power like this; the fulfilment in view may well be Jehoiachin's capitulation to Nebuchadnezzar and Babylon in 597 BC (2 Kings 24:10-12) or Zedekiah's downfall in the siege of 587 BC (2 Kings 25:1-7).[73]

Verse 1 tells us the setting for God's work — complete humiliation. Here is what looks like the total demise of the Davidic dynasty. This is so often where God begins — in our abysmal helplessness.

5:2a
But you, Bethlehem Ephrathah,
  small to be among the clans of Judah…

The opening and emphatic **'But you…'** is the hinge of the passage, leading into the 'hope' section, in contrast to the disastrous 'now' situation of verse 1. The prophet speaks to a town, **'Bethlehem'**, and includes with it what was probably its older name, **'Ephrathah'** (see Gen. 35:19; 48:7). But Micah is doing more than just referring to a town five to six miles south of Jerusalem. The mention of Bethlehem has a slightly ominous ring to it: 'The birth of the Messiah in Bethlehem, and not in Jerusalem the city of David, presupposes that the family of David, out of which it [= the said birth] is to spring, will have lost the throne, and have fallen into poverty.'74 It's as if the quest for the coming king must go all the way back to the 'stump of Jesse' (Isa. 11:1). There will be no royal 'starter kit' still available in Jerusalem; the Davidic dynasty will have been cut off.

The primary significance of Bethlehem is its very insignificance. It is **small to be among the clans** [or, thousands] **of Judah'**. As Laetsch points out, Bethlehem is 'not named among the more than hundred cities allotted to Judah' in Joshua 15:21-63.75 Here then we see a frequent tendency in God's ways, for God is prone to choose the obscure, the insignificant, the lowly, the common, the unnoticed as the very instrument(s) through which he displays the brightest flashes of his glory.

5:2b
… from *you* will come forth for *me*
  [one] to be ruler over Israel;

and his goings forth are from long ago,
  from distant days.

The second part of verse 2 begins with a double emphasis: **'from *you* will come forth for *me*'**. Yahweh is
speaking, and he stresses that this coming ruler will
come forth **'for *me*'**. We easily forget this — that the
coming kingdom is *God's* show and that what matters
is what *God* wants. Yahweh spoke this way to Samuel
when he first sent him to Jesse's farm; he said, 'I have
seen among his sons a king for myself' (1 Sam. 16:1).
It's only one Hebrew syllable (*lî*) but it can knock down
mountains of our idolatry, as does Paul's concise
confession in 1 Corinthians 8:6: '… but for us there is
one God, the Father, from whom are all things, and
we exist *for him*' (emphasis mine).

We will come back to the **'from you'** (Bethlehem).
Note, however, that this coming one will be ruler **'over
Israel'** — not 'in Israel' (as NASB, NRSV, ESV have it),
but 'over' (as in NIV). The combination of the verb
form and following preposition (participle of *māšal* + *bĕ*)
means to 'rule over'.[76] He will rule not simply over
Judah, but over the whole reunited people, north and
south. This reunion of the two 'nations' is a recurring
theme in the prophets (see Isa. 11:13-14; Hosea 1:11;
Jer. 3:18; Ezek. 37:15-22).

But what does the next line mean? **'His goings
forth are from long ago, from distant days.'** One
can pick up a diversity of views in the various translations: 'His origin is from antiquity, from eternity'
(CSB; cf. also NKJV), which suggests the eternal pre-
existence of the coming ruler; or, 'whose origins go
back to the distant past, to the days of old' (NJB; cf.
NRSV), which implies that his roots are in distant
historical time. I support the second option. That does
not mean that I dispute the deity of the Messiah. The
deity of the Messiah in the Old Testament is beyond

dispute as far as I'm concerned.[77] The question is: What does *this text* teach?

I have used **'long ago'** to translate *qedem*. This term can connote eternity when used of God (Deut. 33:27; Ps. 55:19; Hab. 1:12), but more usually refers to events associated with the Exodus (Ps. 74:2,12; 77:11; Isa. 51:9 — please check contexts) and conquest (Ps. 44:1), to the days of David (Neh. 12:46), or to a time years before when Yahweh had announced his 'Cyrus' predictions (Isa. 45:21; 46:10). Micah himself speaks of 'days of *qedem*' (7:20), referring to the times of Abraham and Jacob.

I have used **'from distant days'** to translate 'from days of '*ôlām*'. Once more Micah himself uses this phrase in 7:14, where it refers to the conquest and settlement period (and/or, as some suggest, the days of the empire under David and Solomon). In Amos 9:11 'days of '*ôlām*' refers to the time of David's kingdom; in Isaiah 63:9,11 it alludes to the Exodus period and the time of Moses' leadership. With 'days of' or 'years of' in front of '*ôlām* the phrase points to some distant historical time(s).[78]

Where then does this take us? Back to Bethlehem, I believe. This last line of verse 2 (**'his goings forth'**) is actually simply a kind of confirmation or expansion of the previous line (**'from you will come forth...'**). Many have pointed out the semi-word-play on the verb 'will come forth' and the noun 'goings forth' (both from *yāṣā* '). So the messianic ruler will come forth from 'you' (= Bethlehem), and, in fact, his 'roots' (we might say) go back to 'long ago', to 'distant days' — i.e., to Bethlehem days, the days of David. When Micah speaks of Bethlehem he means not only 'little town' but 'Davidsburg'. He wants to conjure up in our minds the whole episode in 1 Samuel 16 when Yahweh made his choice of David clear, and that in turn should dredge up memories of Yahweh's covenant with David in 2 Samuel 7: 'Your house and your kingdom shall be made sure for ever before me; your throne shall be established for ever' (2 Sam. 7:16). The kingship as Judah knows it in Jerusalem will suffer eclipse (5:1), but Micah takes us back to Bethlehem, to David's days, to the time of Yahweh's choice of David and covenant with David. The future ruler has his roots in that election and covenant. For Micah, 'Bethlehem' means not only 'birthplace' but 'firm promise' as well. The empire *du jour* may cut off the river of Davidic kingship, but it cannot staunch the spring that feeds it.

In this second part of verse 2, then, we see the indefectibility of God's promise. This verse answers questions such as, 'With the royal line defunct (5:1), has Yahweh's judgement demolished Yahweh's promise? Will the tree of Jesse remain a mere stump? Will Nebuchadnezzar falsify the word of God?' The answer is a threefold 'No'. Through no design of mine it is very early on Christmas morning as I write this. The whole family was asleep when I slipped away to my study to work on 'Micah'. And I have found exactly what I need for Christmas: an ancient, defiant, unbreakable promise.[79]

5:3-5a

Therefore he will give them up
 until the time that she who gives birth has given birth
 and the rest of his brothers will return
  along with the sons of Israel.
And he shall stand and act as shepherd
 in the strength of Yahweh,
 in the majesty of the name of Yahweh his God;
and they shall dwell securely,
 for now he will be great to the ends of the earth!
And he shall be peace...

Verse 3 explains how the clear disaster of verse 1 and the bright promises of verse 2 can possibly fit together:

Yahweh will **'give ... up'** the covenant people to severe affliction (cf. 5:1) before the coming ruler is born (5:3) and begins his reign (5:4). Before they ever enjoy the promise of verse 2 they will experience the abandonment of verse 3, and it is crucial for believers in Judah to realize this lest they lose heart. Calvin put it this way:

> Micah proclaims that even the faithful will experience being *given up for a time*. It's as if he were saying, 'My friends, God is going to allow your enemies to afflict you, and you will experience no relief during your sufferings. Why? Because God is going to give you up, as if he could not care less about you. That is why he warns you, that you might be disposed to receive your afflictions with patience.'[80]

So much for the function of verse 3. Now we must tackle its details. Who is the **'she'** who 'gives birth'? Many (e.g., Calvin, Kleinert,[81] von Orelli, Barker, Waltke) are impressed by the use of the same term (*yôlēdâ*, a woman in labour or giving birth) in 4:9-10, where it refers to Daughter Zion, and propose that here too it carries a 'corporate' sense — i.e., Zion, or the remnant of Judah from which the Messiah springs.[82] However, I think it simply refers to the mother of the Messiah (wholly apart from any consideration of Isa. 7:14); if Yahweh gives **'them'** (the nation, including the remnant) up, the 'she' that immediately follows more naturally designates an individual.[83]

And who are **'the rest of his brothers'**, and what is involved in their 'returning'? This part of the verse is difficult and I cannot discuss every commentator's view; I can only set down what seems most feasible to me.

The subject, 'the rest of his brothers', carries some emphasis since it is placed before the verb. I take **'his'** to mean the 'ruler' of verse 2, the Messiah. I assume this refers to a remnant from the Messiah's own tribe, from the 'clans of Judah' (5:2), who survive, or endure, the 'giving up' of the opening line of verse 3. But don't miss the relational category. He is not some isolated Messiah — he has **'brothers'**. Jesus seems to revel in being joined to his people in this way (cf. Rom. 8:29; Heb. 2:11-12,17). He is not only a saving but a *social* Messiah.

This remnant of Judah will return **'along with'** the sons of Israel. The preposition here is *'al*, and English versions usually render it 'to' in this text. Keil, however, holds that 'along with' is better here, a sense it has in Jeremiah 3:18 and Exodus 35:22.[84] The text points to the reunion of the covenant people, always a 'hot topic' for the prophets (Hosea 1:11; 3:5; Isa. 11:12-13; Jer. 31:2-6; Ezek. 37:15-28),[85] and probably to their conversion (**'return'**, *šûb*, may point to a 'return' *to* Yahweh more than *from* exile).[86]

In verse 4 Micah describes the rule of the ruler of verse 2: **'he shall stand and act as shepherd'**. This occurs after the 'giving up' of verse 3; that giving up would last until the birth of the messianic ruler and the reunion and conversion of his people. There is nothing unsteady, hesitant or tentative about his dominance, for he rules **'in the strength of Yahweh, in the majesty of the name of Yahweh his God'**. 'He asserts that God is the one who will sustain this kingdom and government that he gives his Son.'[87] The strength of his rule guarantees the security of his people: **'and they shall dwell securely'**. 'Dwell securely' translates the verb *yāšab*, literally, 'to sit'. Pusey draws attention to the propriety of the two verbs: the Messiah shall **'stand'** (*'āmad*), and his people shall 'sit' (*yāšab*). Because he stands and vigilantly shepherds, they sit and enjoy security.[88]

'For now he will be great' — this is the reason that Messiah's people are secure. Don't miss that particle **'now'** (*'attâ*). Remember how Micah has used that 'now' to introduce the 'down' situations, the disaster times in 4:9,11 and 5:1; those were the 'nasty nows' depicting Yahweh's judgements on them. But here (I shan't use 'now' lest you think it overkill!) Micah reverses all that with a climactic, triumphant 'now'! 'Now he will be great' — and that greatness will be worldwide, **'to the ends of the earth'**. Messiah's reign, then, is mighty, steadying, triumphant and universal. In a word, **'he shall be peace'** (5:5). In the face of the sad 'nows' of our history (4:9,11; 5:1), of the mystery of divine abandonment (5:3) and of the threats from the 'Assyrias' of this age (see the following context), this Shepherd himself is our peace and holds us fast.

Verses 3-5a sketch out the future of God's people. This future will involve, first, *limited affliction* (5:3a). Some time after the birth of this David-to-come, Israel's affliction will come to an end. Though the affliction is grievous, it is not perpetual. It is God's way to place limits on the affliction of his people.

Secondly, this future consists of *restored unity* (5:3b). This takes place some time between the Messiah's birth (5:3) and his consummated rule (5:4).

And *lasting security* (5:4-5a) is the third component in this future. The time comes when Yahweh arises and places his people in the safety for which they long (Ps. 12:5). This is not pie in the sky by and by; this is the security promised to the people of God in the coming kingdom of God and they rightly crave and fervently expect it (Rev. 7:15-17).

Application

Some towns have reputations. In my own country Pigeon Forge, Tennessee, is known for its retail outlets. It is a Mecca for shopping addicts. Belzoni, Mississippi, claims to be the catfish capital of the world (though Savannah, Tennessee, I've discovered, boasts the same). Bethlehem, place of David's residence and anointing (1 Sam. 16:1-13), symbolizes the covenant promise Yahweh made to David (2 Sam. 7:12-16) — that no one will ever finally destroy his dynasty, swallow up his kingdom, or trash his throne. And yet, Micah says, it will nearly come to that; the decimation of the royal line (5:1) and the abandonment of the covenant people (5:3) couldn't make Israel's future look more bleak and hopeless. But there is a small town in Judah that stands for a *stubborn promise* of God, a promise that can never be falsified or terminated, no matter how seemingly beyond help Yahweh's cause appears to be.

In January 1835, Andrew Jackson was walking through the Capitol rotunda and was nearly cut down by a would-be assassin. Richard Lawrence approached the president and levelled a pistol at him, which misfired. Jackson was now coming on, cane raised, to whip his assailant, when Lawrence produced another pistol — which also misfired! Both of these pistols were subsequently fired. Someone estimated the odds of two consecutive misfires at 1 in 125,000.[89] It looked like the end, but it wasn't.

That is often the case in the kingdom of God. And Micah's prophecy reminds us that God's Messiah will be born and God's kingdom will come, not because conditions look optimal, or the world outlook encouraging, but because Yahweh has promised, and nothing and no one can overthrow his will.

What will the Messianic Age be like?
(Micah 5:5-15)

It's very difficult to have a basketball game without baskets, or a library without books, or a police department without — well, police officers. Nor can one have a messianic age without a Messiah. Micah knew that — hence he spoke of the coming messianic ruler in 5:1-4. Let's pull things together a bit. Micah seems to say, 'The glory of 4:1-4 and the salvaging, redeeming and triumph of Zion in 4:6-13 — all this will not happen without the Messiah. He is the centre of it all.' Hence *the presence of the Messiah* is the primary mark of the messianic age (5:1-4). But he will rule over a reunited and secure people (5:3-4). Indeed, as Calvin would say, one cannot think of a king without at the same time thinking of his subjects. That is what Micah does in 5:5-15: he focuses on *the people of the Messiah* as he depicts the messianic age.

Here I want to cheat a bit. I treated the first line of verse 5 as the climax of 5:1-4. And I don't repent of that. However, I also want to drag the opening line of verse 5 into this segment because it helps us to see how to divide up this text describing the messianic age. If we include the whole of verse 5, then four times in verses 5-15 we have segments that begin with the same verb pattern, the conjunction plus *hāyâ* (a perfect, third-person masculine singular form), literally, 'And it shall be' (5:5,7,8,10). An introductory 'And it shall be' (sometimes together with 'in that day', as in 5:10) seems to be an easy way for a prophet to add

extra details or 'footnotes' to a prophecy that he has
already given. Isaiah did this in Isaiah 7:18,21,22,23
(fleshing out what life under an Assyrian scourge
would be like); in Isaiah 11:10,11 (additional pictures
of the Messianic age); and in Isaiah 23:15,17,18 (more
details on the ruin of Tyre). Micah is doing that here;
with his added *wĕhāyâ* sections he is filling out the
picture of what it will be like when the Messiah reigns
(5:1-4). Micah's second and third uses of the verb
form in the opening lines of verses 7 and 8 are obviously parallel (though paradoxical), so I keep them
together in one combined segment. This gives us three
sections, verses 5-6, 7-9 and 10-15, describing what
the messianic age will be like.

5:5-6
And he shall be peace.
Assyria — when he enters our land
    and when he sets foot on our fortifications,
then we shall raise up seven shepherds against him,
    yes, eight leaders of men.
And they shall shepherd the land of Assyria with the sword
    and the land of Nimrod at its entrances,
and he shall deliver from Assyria
    when he enters our land
    and when he sets foot on our border.

When Messiah reigns (5:4-5) you can name your worst
fear without swallowing your teeth. **'Assyria'** stands
in stark isolation at the opening of the second part of
verse 5. Assyria was the international scourge *du jour*
in Micah's own time. However, I think Micah uses
'Assyria' here not in a strictly historical sense, but in a
broadly representative sense — i.e., as standing for
any and all enemies that can threaten God's people.[90]
In verse 6 the parallel to **'land of Assyria'** is **'land of
Nimrod'**, which points us back to Genesis 10:8-12,
where Nimrod's 'sphere of influence' included both

southern and northern Mesopotamian sites — i.e., both 'Babylonia' and 'Assyria'. Hence Micah seems to use 'Assyria' in a more comprehensive sense, one not confined to eighth-century BC dimensions. When 'Assyria' comes, Micah insists that Messiah's people will raise **'seven shepherds'** against the invader, **'yes, eight leaders of men'**, as if to say, 'We'll have a full battery of leaders — even more than enough.'[91] Their success will be not only defensive but offensive; they will not only defend but dominate: **'they shall shepherd** [i.e., rule] **the land of Assyria with the sword'**, etc. (5:6).[92] By depicting both defensive success (5:5) and offensive dominance (5:6) Micah conveys the idea of 'complete victory'. However, this victory must not be chalked up to these 'shepherds': Micah's second line in verse 6 begins with a singular verb: **'And he shall deliver from Assyria.'** He refers back to the one who will be peace in the first line of verse 5. The messianic king himself is the true deliverer.

Some may wonder how the coming king can be called 'the One of Peace' (Andersen/Freedman) in the first line of verse 5 when the rest of the verse and the whole of the following one seem to bristle with conflict. If we are perplexed about this, it simply means that there is an aspect of peace that we have not understood. Gideon can help us. When Gideon was pursuing the kings of Midian he had asked the men of Penuel for provisions for his troops. They had refused and Gideon told them, 'When I come again in peace [šālôm], I will pull down this tower' (Judg. 8:9). He meant, 'After I have thrashed and trounced these Midianite kings, I am going to deal with you.' He will come in peace after he has won the victory. **'Peace'**, then, is almost equivalent to victory. Peace does not mean one never fights; peace is what comes after you win the fight! It is not some anaemic serenity; if there is serenity, it's because the opposition has been liquidated. The New Testament agrees: 'The God of *peace* will soon *crush* Satan under your feet' (Rom. 16:20, emphasis added).

5:7-9

And the remnant of Jacob shall be
  in the midst of many peoples
  like dew from Yahweh,
  like showers on grass
  — something that does not look eagerly for man
  or place hope in the sons of men.
And the remnant of Jacob shall be
  among the nations, in the midst of many peoples
  like a lion among beasts of the forest,
  like a young lion among flocks of sheep
  — when it passes through and tramples down and tears
    up
  there is none to deliver.
Your hand will be lifted up against your adversaries,
  and all your enemies will be cut off.

What superb news! There *is* a **'remnant of Jacob'**, a true people of God, that will endure exile (4:9-10) and being 'given up' (5:3) and will thrive in the messianic age. In these verses Micah predicts the impact this preserved and faithful people will have worldwide (note **'in the midst of many peoples'**, in both verses 7 and 8, with **'among the nations'** added in verse 8). He gives two pictures of how this remnant will affect 'many peoples', pictures that in my view are intentionally paradoxical.

The first picture appears in verse 7. The remnant will be **'like dew from Yahweh, like showers on grass'**. 'Dew' (*ṭal*) can mean what we call dew, but can also include light rain or drizzle.[93] The semi-synonym *rĕbîbîm* refers to light showers or drizzle.[94] The image connotes the refreshing, revitalizing effect of dew and showers, and hence of the remnant. Yahweh's people will in some way have a renewing and beneficial impact on the nations.[95]

The last part of verse 7 seems to mean that this refreshment is 'not at all dependent on the doings and strivings of men', but on the grace of God alone.[96] This was implied previously when the text said the remnant would be 'like dew *from Yahweh*'. So it is supernatural, a gift of grace.

Verse 8 paints the second picture: the remnant will be **'like a lion ... like a young lion'**. The **'beasts of the forest'** and **'flocks of sheep'** do not denote wild animals versus tame ones, but are larger and smaller domesticated animals respectively.[97] One can imagine how appetizing a young lion would find a flock of helpless sheep. Micah pictures the hopeless scenario in a series of three violent verbs (**'passes through ... tramples down ... tears up'**) followed by the statement: **'There is none to deliver.'**

We have some options in our understanding of verse 9. First, the imperfect-tense verbs can be either statements (indicatives), as I have translated them, or wishes (subjunctives) — 'May', or 'let your hand be lifted up,' etc. — either is legitimate here. Secondly, the **'your'** could refer to either God or the 'lion-remnant' of verse 8. In this context I think it more natural to take the prophet as making a confident declaration to the remnant.[98]

Some interpreters are queasy about seeing the remnant in this two-edged way, as both benefit and bane to the nations. So they labour to turn the dew / rain simile into a harmful, more 'lionesque' sense.[99] But this is strained — why can't Micah be at least as sophisticated as we are and deliberately use paradox? We may be perplexed over how the remnant could both refresh and ravage among many peoples. But perhaps Micah wants us to *think*. Whether it holds the specific answer or not, Jesus' scenario of the sheep and the goats in Matthew 25:31-46 demonstrates the

way his people become either a bane or a blessing for
the nations. There the nations are judged on how they
treat Jesus' people, his 'brothers', as he calls them (v.
40). The way they 'handle' Jesus' people can determine
the blessing or blasting of the nations. So why should
Micah 5:7-9 be so difficult?

5:10-15
And it shall be in that day, says Yahweh,
that I shall cut off your horses from among you
    and destroy your chariots;
and I shall cut off the cities of your land
    and tear down all your fortresses;
and I shall cut off sorceries from your hand,
    and you will no more have any diviners;
and I shall cut off your carved images
    and your stone pillars from your midst,
and you will no longer bow down to the work of your hands;
and I shall rip out your Asherah poles from your midst,
    and exterminate your cities.
And I shall carry out — with anger and rage — vengeance
    on the nations who have not obeyed.

Here is Micah's last 'snapshot' of the messianic age (at
least in this context). He introduces it with *wĕhāyâ*,
'And it shall be' with an added **'in that day'**; he
means, 'These are the conditions that will prevail in
that day.' By 'in that day' he refers — according to his
governing context — to the Messiah's reign (5:4).
    Yahweh's oracle, at least from the second line of
verse 10 through to verse 13, comes in a sledgehammer style. At the end of verse 9 Micah had used a
passive form of the verb *kārat*: '... and all your enemies
will be cut off. Yahweh, as it were, picks up that verb
and uses it in its first-person causative form four
times (5:10,11,12,13) as he hammers home how he
will purge his people of the idolatrous rubbish they
have accumulated. In these verses he details the

destructive work he must do in order to produce a holy people.[100]

First, Yahweh says, 'I shall cut down *your military securities*' (5:10-11). Horses and chariots were the attack helicopters and tanks of the eighth century BC. Like any nation, Judah was forever tempted to place her hope in her defence budget (cf. Ps. 20:7; 33:16-17; Isa. 31:1). In verse 11 Yahweh fills out the picture — not only will he cut down their offensive weaponry (horses, chariots, 5:10), but their defensive protection (cities, fortresses) as well. When enemies invaded, people would take refuge within the walled cities and fortified places (see, e.g., Jer. 35:11).[101] Israel will have to trust Yahweh alone, for he will totally eliminate all their favourite safety devices and level every cherished place of refuge.

Secondly, Yahweh says, 'I shall cut down *your religious substitutes*' (5:12-14). So sorceries and divination, or soothsaying, will bite the dust. Sorcery tried to control the future; divination sought to discern the future ahead of time in order to gain advantage by such knowledge.[102] In paganism the gods and goddesses came from the same 'stuff' as the world and so were not all-sufficient and omnipotent. Hence man (and sometimes the gods themselves, according to the myths) resorted to magic in order to enlist the area of 'power' beyond that held by the gods themselves and to which even the gods were subject[103] — a great opportunity for control freaks. Micah may have used the terms **'sorceries'** and **'diviners'** here in order to suggest the whole gamut of pagan hanky-panky that refuses to be content with the mere word of Yahweh spoken through the prophets (see Deut. 18:9-13, for the whole catalogue of pagan perversions, and the following context, where the gift of prophecy stands against them).

Yahweh will also take out their **'carved images'** (5:13) and the pagan paraphernalia at their centres of syncretistic worship — the 'standing stones' (5:13), representing male Baal, and the wooden Asherah poles (5:14), representing his female counterpart.[104] Sorceries, diviners, carved images, standing stones, Asherah poles — there's quite a pile for extermination. And it's what we can call a loving destruction with a transformational intent: **'and you will no longer bow down to the work of your hands'** (5:13).[105]

We might pause here to say that what Yahweh attacks in this passage is *a lack of contentment* in his people. They are not satisfied with his mere promise of security (5:10-11). They are not content with the limits of Yahweh's revelation — they want secrets from the magical 'arts'; they want to be able to take control of their circumstances; mere commandments are not enough — they want secrets for success (5:12). The simplicity of Yahweh's worship grates on them — they want the added thrill of visible likenesses (5:13). Nor are they content with Yahweh's provision — they want to *do* something; they want to contribute to the drama of fertility — hence the pillars and poles, the Baal-and-Asherah show and participating in the sex side-show at the shrine and 'doing their part' to nudge fertility into a higher gear. They — and we — want security that is more tangible, faith that is more manipulative, worship that is more impressive. Somehow it is so difficult to be satisfied with the fountain of living waters! (Jer. 2:13).

Yahweh has fired a veritable volley of violent verbs in this section: **'cut off'**, **'destroy'**, **'tear down'**, **'rip out'**, **'exterminate'**. But he will do all of this in order to have a purged people. Calvin has put it well:

> On the surface, Micah employs a harsh sentence here in proclaiming that God will pull down walls and strongholds, destroy weapons, and take away their horses and chariots. But Micah is introducing, rather, an exhortation that

ought to make us rejoice. And why? Because it signals that God intends to remove any impediment that might cause us to turn aside from coming to him, thus disposing us to render ourselves obedient to him with all our heart, choosing to make God our sole good, joy, and glory.[106]

And we ought to be ecstatic over that!

Now we must not forget verse 15. Yahweh will severely sanctify his own people (5:10-14), but he will also **'carry out ... vengeance'** on the nations who have not obeyed (5:15). In our soft-headed, emotion-driven Western culture a verse like this makes people go ballistic. 'Vengeance' — as if all the nonsense they have heard about the Old Testament is true! But 'vengeance' (*nāqām*) is good; it is what ought to be.[107] Popular imagination takes vengeance as synonymous with viciousness, nastiness, meanness and vindictiveness. In the Bible, it's not. That doesn't mean it's pleasant. But vengeance (from God) is what is needed in order for justice to be done. Read Psalm 94 and you will start praying for it yourself. The only sure hope Yahweh's people have is that Yahweh is 'avenging' (Nahum 1:2, where the word comes three times!) — therefore, they can count on his putting things right and doling out justice to their enemies. The nations **'who have not obeyed'** are the rebellious nations, the nations of 4:11-13 who reject Yahweh and hate Zion — the opposite camp from those who come hungering and thirsting for Yahweh's words in the latter days (4:1-4).

Application

Micah portrays the sort of people the Messiah will have — and indeed the kind of people he *ought* to have even now. He has a *secure and protected* people (5:5-6). Because the Messiah is the strong Shepherd who rules to the ends of the earth (5:4), his people are secure — as secure as those the Good Shepherd describes: 'And I give to them eternal life, and they will never, ever perish, and no one shall rip them out of my hand' (John 10:28). So one can name one's worst fear — it may be 'Assyria' (5:5), or Alzheimer's — and still say, 'and he shall deliver' (5:6) in the same breath.

But they are also a *refreshing and dangerous* people (5:7-9). Christ's people carry a double edge; they may have a 'precipitation' effect (dew, rain, 5:7) or a 'predatory' effect (lion, young lion, 5:8) among the nations; they may refresh or ravage, renew or ruin. One sees traces of this even in the present age. For example, multiple bounties come to our world because of Christ's people. On one occasion Spurgeon made a telling point in debate with an agnostic who was pooh-poohing the pastor's faith. Spurgeon pointed out the utter failure of any unbelievers' organizations to take on any sustained help to thousands of needy around them in contrast to the social and compassionate ministries of Christians. Then, in a paraphrase of Elijah's challenge on Mt Carmel (1 Kings 18:24), Spurgeon closed the conversation with: 'The God who answereth by orphanages, let him be God!'[108] So, let the Marxists show us the hospitals they've built, the orphanages they've provided for African children suffering from AIDS. Do missionaries or Marxists build schools and medical clinics? Do drug-running guerrillas dig wells so that threatened people can have safe water?

Messiah's people can also have a devastating impact even in this age. Louis XIV revoked the Edict of Nantes in 1685, once more allowing the persecution of Protestants (Huguenots) in France; hundreds of thousands of France's most productive people emigrated, gutting France's economy but proving a welcome boon to Holland, England and Germany. One might argue that France has still not recovered from Louis' stupid and bigoted decree.[109] The Messiah has put nations on notice (Matt. 25:40, in context): 'Your treatment of my people reveals you and determines your blessing or your blasting.' Maybe we should print some signs: 'Danger — Beware of sheep!'

Finally, Messiah is going to have a *purified and faithful* people (5:10-15). This seems almost too much to believe, whether one meets it in the Old Testament, as here, or in the New, as in Ephesians 5:26-27. Knowing the church as I do, I have always wondered about that 'without spot or wrinkle' bit. The church often seems more like a shrivelled prune than a radiant bride. But Christ will change all that. He will do all he must — cut off, pull down, rip up, exterminate, in order that 'he might sanctify her' (Eph. 5:26). He is going to take a Bible-denying, love-lacking, gripe-producing, trivia-loving people, purge them, and turn them into full-blooded, righteousness-loving worshippers, who have been stripped of their idols and are greedy for holiness. Will you be numbered among them?

3. Through judgement to pardon
Micah 6:1 – 7:20

The Lord's litigation
(Micah 6:1-8)

Now Yahweh drags Israel into court. His case contains accusation (6:3-5), satire (6:6-7) and declaration (6:8). We also enter a new (and final) major division of the book at this point. The command to **'hear'** (imperative plural) in 6:1 parallels the same structural marker in 1:2 and 3:1. Once more this last section (chs. 6 – 7) begins with a negative segment (6:1 – 7:7) followed by a positive (7:8-20), and so I have dubbed the whole piece 'through judgement to pardon'.

One hears three 'voices' in verses 1-8: that of Yahweh, primarily (6:1-5), of a would-be worshipper (6:6-7) and of the prophet (6:8). If we break up the opening section into two, we can follow the movement in the text: first, assembling (6:1-2); second, arguing (6:3-5); third, responding (6:6-7); and, fourth, correcting (6:8). We cannot be sure about the precise historical setting for this passage. It might be the reign of Ahaz (735–715 BC, Andersen and Freedman), or Sennacherib's siege in Hezekiah's time (701 BC, apparently the view of Waltke), or the early reign of Manasseh, when all was headed to wickedness (Gary Smith). If forced to vote, I would go for the first option, but we simply don't know.

6:1-2
Hear now what Yahweh is saying:
(Rise, press the case before the mountains,
and let the hills hear your voice.)
Hear, O mountains, Yahweh's case
— and [you] enduring ones,
    [you] foundations of the earth;
for Yahweh has a case with his people
and with Israel he will prove himself right.

I have placed part of verse 1 in brackets because it
seems to be an aside that Yahweh addresses to Micah.
The verbs **'rise'** (*qûm*) and **'press the case'** (*rîb*) are
singular verbs; the **'your'** in **'your voice'** is singular
as well.[1] So, after the initial call to **'hear'** (imperative
plural), it's as though Yahweh turns aside to address
and stir up his prophet to serve as prosecutor.

Micah then calls on the mountains to hear Yah-
weh's **'case'** (the root, *rîb*, occurs three times in verses
1-2, once as a verb, 6:1; twice as a noun, 6:2) — as
the aggrieved party, Yahweh, is bringing his complaint
and accusation against Israel.[2] The mountains are
'witnesses', since they are **'enduring ones'** that have
been around for aeons and could therefore vouch for
all that has gone on, so to speak.[3] How they can be
'foundations of the earth' is a bit puzzling; perhaps
the image is akin to Jonah's going down to the 'ex-
tremities [apparently = 'bottoms'] of the mountains' in
his deep-sea plunge (Jonah 2:6); if the bottoms of the
mountains are there they might be thought to be very
foundational.

The very last line of verse 2, 'and with/against
Israel he will establish what is right for himself' (as
Waltke translates it) seems to go beyond simply repeating the gist of the previous line (namely, that
Yahweh has a **'case with his people'**); it seems to
point to the outcome of the case. The verb is *yākaḥ*,
with the sense 'to determine what is right'. Here it is

in a reflexive form and, as Waltke argues, would mean, 'He will establish what is right for himself.'[4] This suggests that he will get to the bottom of things, even that he will prove himself right (reflected in my translation).

6:3-5

'My people, what have I done to you?
And how have I wearied you?
Witness against me!
For I brought you up from the land of Egypt,
and from the house of slaves I ransomed you;
then I sent before you Moses, Aaron and Miriam.
My people, remember what Balak king of Moab counselled
and what Balaam son of Beor answered him
— [remember] from Shittim to Gilgal —
that you may know the righteous acts of Yahweh.'

One can understand verse 2 as Yahweh speaking, or, more likely, as Micah introducing Yahweh's words. In verses 3-5, however, we have Yahweh himself addressing Israel. Twice he calls them **'my people'** (6:3,5) — he is not so much accusing as appealing. Yahweh is courteous even when he drags Israel into court! And he wants to know what charge Israel can lodge against him. What has he done to them? In particular, how has he wearied (lā'â) them? This verb signifies being worn out or exhausted (Job 16:7; Jer. 12:5) or, with a more emotional tinge, exasperated (Job 4:5; Isa. 7:13). The cognate noun connotes hardship (e.g., Exod. 18:8; Num. 20:14; Neh. 9:32) that wears down; in fact, worship could be such a hardship or 'pain' that priests regarded it as so much 'weariness' or 'tedium' (Mal. 1:13).[5] So Yahweh wants to know how he has worn them out, how he has been such a drag, or proven so boring.

Yahweh does not miss a beat but plunges straight into his 'defence'. I take the **'for'** at the beginning of verse 4 as causal — Yahweh is setting out the reasons why he has not wearied Israel. He cites the astounding record of his **'righteous acts'** (6:5).

The first is *redemption:* **'I brought you up from the land of Egypt, and from the house of slaves I ransomed you'** (6:4).[6] Note the **'you'**. It assumes the unity of God's people. Actually, Yahweh had brought up Moses' generation from Egypt; yet here he speaks to Micah's generation and says, 'I brought *you* up from Egypt.' The Exodus may have taken place 700 years before but, in one sense, Micah's contemporaries were there. In the words of Allen, there is no 'chronological chasm' between ancient event and contemporary people.[7] Yahweh's redemption does not expire by some 'sell-by' date.

To catch the argument one has almost to pretend that Yahweh is firing questions at the prophet's hearers: 'Was liberation boring? Does release from years of servitude make you yawn? Is the Exodus story wearisome? All that about raising up a deliverer (Exod. 1 – 4); crushing opposition (Exod. 5 – 12); rescuing at the sea, with Pharaoh's army attacking from behind and a sea in front blocking escape (Exod. 14) — do you find that all terribly tedious?'

Yahweh's second righteous act is provision of *leadership*: **'then I sent before you Moses, Aaron and Miriam'** (6:4). Moses was unique in his mediatorial capacity (cf. Exod. 32 – 34) and in receiving intimate and direct revelation from Yahweh (Num. 12:7-8); Aaron served as high priest, overseeing Israel's worship; and Miriam exercised prophetic and liturgical gifts (Exod. 15:20-21; Num. 12:2 — the affirmation in the latter text is true even if spoken in envy). Samuel spoke of Moses and Aaron's leadership as Yahweh's gracious gift (1 Sam. 12:6-8; see also Ps. 77:20; 105:26-27). Here then it is as if Yahweh asks, 'Are you upset because I didn't leave you to wander aimlessly? Would you have preferred to go round in the wilderness like sheep without a shepherd, like helpless toddlers abandoned in a giant supermarket?' Clearly, Yahweh does not redeem and then refuse leadership and direction, which would only lead to another kind of bondage.

Yahweh also gave *protection* in peril: **'remember what Balak king of Moab counselled and what Balaam son of Beor answered him'** (6:5). This picks up the story of Numbers 22 – 24. Balak **'counselled'** Balaam to put a spell on Israel for him, so that he might defeat them (Num. 22:6). But Yahweh restrained Balaam (Num. 22:12,20,35,38), and Balaam could only tell Balak that, being held in Yahweh's vicelike grip, he dare not curse the people Yahweh had blessed (Num. 23:8; 24:13). 'Do you remember that?', Yahweh seems to say. 'Was I wrong to stonewall that money-grubbing diviner and keep him from putting his hokey-pokey on you?'

The next bit of verse 5 reads simply, **'from Shittim to Gilgal'**, which seems abrupt and rough. But the verb 'remember' (*zākar*) probably does double duty here — that is, it is only written once, but is to be understood twice.[8] They were not only to remember the conniving of Balak and Balaam, but also the events as they travelled from Shittim to Gilgal. Shittim was Israel's location before she crossed the Jordan (Num. 25:1; Josh. 2:1; 3:1) and Gilgal her headquarters post-Jordan (Josh. 4:19). 'From Shittim to Gilgal' means all that happened in the course of Israel's crossing the Jordan River and entering the land in Joshua 3 – 4. On the basis of that passage we could dub Yahweh's fourth 'righteous act' *excitement* over a promise fulfilled. The timing was impossible — it was spring and the Jordan was in full flood (Josh. 3:15); the story is nail-biting — as soon as the priests' feet touch the water the Jordan is 'cut off', and as soon as they step out of the water (4:18) the river comes back with a whoosh. It was a veritable pins-and-needles episode. One might imagine Yahweh arguing his case: 'Was that boring? Did I fail to sustain your interest there? Didn't you reach for the antacids? Did my cliff-hanging providence not stimulate you?'

Yahweh makes a point of taking them through this review of grace so that they might **'know the righteous acts of Yahweh'** (6:5) — not merely his 'saving acts' (as ESV) but his **'righteous acts'** (*ṣidqôt*), or 'acts of vindication', in which he righteously acted to put things right for an oppressed people (see Judg. 5:11; 1 Sam. 12:7-8; Ps. 103:6).[9] Israel is to **'know'** these acts, not merely as pieces of data, but as the combined evidence of his grace that claims their repentance and obedience. To **'remember'** involves the same; it is not mere recollection; remembrance refers to what grips you and moves you and drives you.[10]

Before pressing on, let us pause a moment to ponder verses 3-5 as a whole. First, think what Micah's hearers may have thought of Yahweh's evidence. (Yes, I'm inserting a bit of imagination here.) What is the problem with these 'righteous acts'? What objections might the prophet's audience have had with them? They might have said, 'Why, these are such *old* actions. We are the chic 730 BC generation and Micah takes us back 700 years. Why not something more recent? Why is he so traditional rather than contemporary?' In one sense, it is a good question: why is Yahweh always dragging his people back over the timeline and teaching them *history* in order to sustain their faith, crack their apathy, rebuke their boredom and shame their faithlessness?

Second, a partial answer to that question arises from the implicit logic of verses 3-5. The argument runs like this: 'If Yahweh pried Israel from Pharaoh's grip, shielded them from the dark arts in Moab, and dammed up a rampaging Jordan, then isn't he able to carry them through any peril history can throw at

them?[11] Can a contemporary superpower like Assyria
really prove too difficult for him to handle?'

6:6-7
With what shall I come to meet Yahweh?
[With what] shall I bow myself before God Most High?
Shall I come to meet him with burnt offerings?
With calves a year old?
Will Yahweh take pleasure in thousands of rams,
   in ten thousand torrents of oil?
Shall I give my firstborn [for] my rebellion,
the fruit of my body [for] the sin of my soul?

Now we hear the voice of a would-be worshipper,
mediated through the prophet. We need not bother
with whether these verses were once an 'entrance
liturgy' — in this context they function as a proposed
response to Yahweh's recital of grace in verses 3-5.
The worshipper suggests several responses, all liturgical, and in an ascending scale of costliness. As Micah
puts the words in the worshipper's mouth he exposes
the latter's wrong-headedness and yet at the same
time captures his attitude.

So how should one approach Yahweh? With burnt
offerings? With calves a year old? (6:6). Unlike a peace
offering, with its ensuing meal (Lev. 3:1-17; 7:15-18),
a burnt offering was completely consumed on the altar
(cf. Lev. 1:9); the worshipper got none of it. And year-
old calves had shekels written all over them — in the
sense that they had had to be cared for and fed for a
whole year when they could have been sacrificed any
time seven days after birth (Lev. 22:27).[12] Note that
both nouns (**'burnt offerings'** and **'calves'**) are plurals — this worshipper is not offering a stingy sample,
but a whole batch.

If Yahweh is not impressed with mere costly worship, will he be pleased with extravagant worship?
(6:7). What if, copying the example of David (1 Chr.

29:21) or Solomon (1 Kings 8:63), one were to offer thousands of rams? Olive oil accompanied offerings (e.g., the daily burnt offering, Exod. 29:40, and the grain offerings in Lev. 2) and was a commodity to be tithed (Deut. 12:17).[13] A 'torrent' (*naḥal*) refers to a wadi or seasonal stream, perhaps bone-dry in summer but a raging torrent in the rainy season. So would Yahweh delight in **'ten thousand torrents of oil'**?

Or will only the ultimate satisfy Yahweh? Is it *human* sacrifice I must give? The suggestion nearly takes one's breath away. The grammar is very stark in the second half of verse 7; literally, the text reads, 'my first-born my rebellion, fruit of my body sin of my soul', or 'life'. Micah simply puts the terms side by side with no preposition between or connecting them (such as I have supplied in the translation above). It's as if the prophet wants to force the hearer / reader to think through the relationship between these separate items. What we must *not* do is dismiss all this as very theoretical, as if Micah is simply using hyperbole to express the conceivable acme of human devotion — a sort of literary device for effect. No, there had already been a king of Judah in Micah's time who had reached this abyss — Ahaz (2 Kings 16:2-3). Others would ape him (e.g., Manasseh, 2 Kings 21:6; cf. 2 Kings 23:10). Micah was not preaching in some hypothetical dreamworld.[14]

6:8
He has told you, O man, what is good.
And what is Yahweh demanding from you
    except doing justice,
       loving mercy,
       and walking carefully with your God?

Here is the prophet's 'not that, but this' correction to the liturgical folly of verses 6-7. Micah says that a right response to Yahweh's marvellous grace is *clear*

(**'He has told you, O man'**), *simple* (**'what ... except...'**, cf. Deut. 10:12-13), *social* (**'doing'** *mišpaṭ*, **'loving'** *ḥesed*) and *reverent* (**'walking carefully with your God'**). Micah is not charting out the way of salvation; he is reasserting how those who are objects of God's grace (6:3-5) are to live and respond to their God.[15] And he begins by saying there is nothing mystical or esoteric — no guesswork — about this matter, for Yahweh **'has told you'** what he wants — that is, he has already made it clear in the Law and the Prophets. He is not looking for frenzied activities, but for a faithful life (cf. 1 Sam. 15:22-23; Isa. 1:10-17).

If we ask what **'doing justice'** involves, Micah might say that he himself has already told us. As Gary Smith says, 'When people in Micah's audience forcibly confiscate other people's land or possessions (Micah 2:1-2,8-9), treat people inhumanely (3:1-2), and selfishly cheat others so that their financial position will be enhanced (3:9-11), these are unjust social relationships.'[16] Doing justice means not perpetrating injustice like that. **'Loving mercy'** goes beyond that, **'mercy'** here being *ḥesed*, faithful or unfailing love. John Mackay captures the sense when he says that loving mercy adds to doing justice 'principally the idea of willingness and delight in acting toward one's fellows with the fidelity and consideration God requires'. He goes on to say that 'it is not an irksome performance of an imposed duty, but a glad and spontaneous action'.[17] So Micah points to the attitude that must drive the action. We are not merely to do justice, but to delight in doing it.

The adverb in the last line is a bit tricky. It is the infinitive absolute of *ṣānaʻ*, which apparently means to be modest, humble, careful.[18] The cognate adjective occurs in Proverbs 11:2 in contrast to one who is arrogant, presumptuous and full of himself. Either **'carefully'** or 'humbly' seems to fit here. Note, however, that Micah speaks of walking carefully **'with**

your God'. Clearly he has in mind those who at least profess having a relationship with Yahweh, those already belonging to the covenant people. This tells us that verse 8 is not a programme for works-salvation but a pattern for covenant living. And he speaks of **'walking'** with your God, which points to a life of ongoing communion and fellowship (cf. Gen. 5:22,24), rather than to sporadic visits to a divine emergency room.[19]

Application

This text places two demands upon us: first, to remember the righteous acts of the Lord (6:3-5); and, second, to make the proper response to the Lord (6:6-8).

Christian believers can update the list of Yahweh's 'righteous acts'. They now include that Christ died (and so guilt is lifted since 'he himself carried our sins in his body on the tree', 1 Peter 2:24); that Christ rose (and so 'abolished death', 2 Tim. 1:10); that Christ reigns (and so we are not under any bondage, for he has supremacy over every benign and malign power, Eph. 1:20-23), that Christ intercedes (and so keeps us from falling away, Luke 22:32); that Christ will come again (and so history is going somewhere, which means that life has purpose and 'drive', Acts 1:11). When we too-often jaded Christians gather before the communion table, does Jesus have to come and say, 'Is this boring? Have I failed to interest you? Have I not stretched your mind, stirred your gratitude, excited your wonder, met your real needs? Was the cross not dramatic enough for you? Does the empty tomb make you yawn?'

We must also not feel smug when we read verses 6-7, for Christians have their own equivalent response. The thinking behind Israel's defective response was: 'God wants to see evidence of my commitment, and the way I show that is by intensifying my religious devotion and activity.' We are not into calves or rams, but may lose ourselves in a ceaseless round of Bible conferences, missions conferences, marriage seminars, singles' retreats, youth ski trips, college or prison ministries and church prayer vigils. We can rigidly follow our Christian guru of choice in rearing our children, plug our church into holding services in the local nursing home and organize a 'Christian' soccer league in our community. On and on it goes; the thought of a night without church activity causes acid indigestion. Not that all these are bad things. But why do we think we have to be so frantic? Why do we have this hypertensive view of the Christian life? Why do we think God wants us to organize more Christian things to do?

The curses are coming
(Micah 6:9-16)

This passage is riddled with minor difficulties, and I may not solve all of them correctly. But let's avoid one fundamental mistake at the start — forgetting that the section is closely tied to verses 1-8. A shift in literary form does not have to mean a break in the flow of thought. So here is the big picture in Micah 6:

1. The righteous acts of Yahweh (especially 6:3-5)
2. The clear requirement of Yahweh (6:6-8)
3. The just judgement of Yahweh (6:9-16)

The judgement of Yahweh is coming (6:9-16) because the requirement of Yahweh (6:6-8) has not been met. Attentive readers will note how verses 10-12 provide an exegesis of the demand for justice and mercy in verse 8, even though they show that this demand has been ignored. Hence the curses for covenant disobedience are on their way (6:13-15). It is time for judgement to begin at the house of God.

6:9
The voice of Yahweh calls to the city
— and fearing your name is sound wisdom.
Give heed to the rod — and who has appointed it?

This verse is the prophet's heading for Yahweh's speech in verses 10-16 (I take the first-person singular pronouns in 6:10-16 to refer to Yahweh). Micah

adds a little worshipful aside after he announces
Yahweh's voice: **'and fearing your name is sound
wisdom'**. Opinions differ whether the verb is 'fear' or
'see / regard'. The Hebrew words are very similar. 'See'
is actually in the traditional text and it could be taken
as: 'Whoever regards your name [shows] sound wisdom.' But one change of a vowel point (vowels were
not in the original Hebrew text) yields **'fearing'**, which
seems to fit better. The **'name'** refers to all that one is
and represents. When Nathaniel queried whether
anything good could come out of Nazareth (John
1:46), he was indicating his low opinion of all that
'Nazareth' was and stood for! Fearing Yahweh's 'name'
means having a trembling trust for all that his name
represents — all that Yahweh is and says.

Figuring out the last line of verse 9 is a tricky
business. Some emend the text and pull in the first
word of verse 10, which yields, 'Hear, O tribe and
assembly of the city' (NRSV; Waltke). The noun *matteh*
can mean 'tribe' or 'rod'. My translation is close to the
NIV here. **'Rod'** as an instrument of punishment
could refer to the Assyrians (cf. Isa. 10). However,
there is a gender glitch in this translation: it's a bit
odd if **'it'** refers to 'rod', since 'it' is feminine in the
Hebrew, while 'rod' is a masculine noun (though
Brown, Driver and Briggs suggest that *matteh* is masculine everywhere but here!).[20] Still, I think our translation is about the best we can do at this point.

6:10-12

'Can I still forget the treasures of wickedness
    in the house of the wicked,
and the skimpy ephah that is cursed?
Can I be in the clear [if I forget] the scales of wickedness
    and the bag containing deceitful weights?
Her rich men are full of violence
and her residents speak lies;
yes, their tongue is nothing but deceit in their mouth.'

The first part of verse 10 can be translated, 'Are there yet treasures of wickedness in the house of the wicked?' However, the second word in the text, *ha'iš*, looks like a parallel verb to **'Can I be in the clear...?'** in the opening line of verse 11. It may be derived from *nšh*, 'to forget'.[21] Hence I translate, **'Can I still forget...?'** Here, in the words of Allen, we meet the Lord of the shopping centre and trade mart. 'Can I forget,' he says, 'the wealth you have amassed from cheating people?'

Unscrupulous merchants had their ways — the **'skimpy ephah'**, for example. Grain sits in an 'ephah' basket at the market awaiting a purchaser. Maybe it looks like a full ephah (about twenty-two litres, or five gallons' worth) but perhaps there is a false bottom in the basket (I don't know this for sure — I'm just imagining how I would try to do it if I were so inclined) and when the dishonest seller pours the grain into the buyer's sack, it's an ephah minus ten per cent.[22] Since no one from the Department of Agriculture was going around checking matters, some of these merchants had another bag of tricks — the stone weights they carried around (6:11). These turned their scales into **'scales of wickedness'**. A buyer might place a certain weight of silver in one pan of the scales. The merchant had in his 'weight' bag a couple of stones that both had the same exterior marking on them, but one was noticeably heavier than the other. He puts the heavier one onto the other pan of the scales and, of course, the buyer then has to add more silver to the 'inadequate' amount he had already supplied.

This all flew in the teeth of the Law (Lev. 19:35-36; Deut. 25:13-16) and the Prophets (e.g., Amos 8:4-6). But business is bu$ine$$! And in verse 11 Yahweh simply says, 'Can I be in the clear if I ignore that and let it pass?'

'Her' in the phrase **'her rich men'** (6:12) refers to Jerusalem, the city Yahweh is addressing (6:9). The upper classes there trample on both law and people as they want, but it's not only the violence of the rich that constitutes the disaster; it's also the falsehood of the populace. The latter **'speak lies'**, and they do so with ungodly consistency, for their tongues are **'nothing but deceit'** (6:12). Corruption is total, affecting both the **'rich'** at the top and the **'residents'** at large: the rich can trample on people; the rest can deceive them; and so, 'from the sole of the foot even to the head, there is no soundness in it' (Isa. 1:6).

6:13-15
'And so I also shall make you sick, striking you down,
devastating [you] on account of your sins.
You will eat — and not be satisfied,
but your hunger will haunt you;
and what you remove you will not preserve,
and what you do preserve I will give to the sword.
You will sow — and will not harvest;
you will tread olives — and not anoint yourself with oil,
tread grapes — and not drink wine.'

After describing the offences (6:10-12), Yahweh announces the judgement (6:13-15). The **'I'** in the opening line of verse 13 is emphatic — 'I on my part', in contrast to the rich power-brokers and lying residents of Jerusalem. Though the verb is in the perfect tense, it is to be translated as a future (**'shall make you sick'**).[23] The rest of verse 13 fleshes out what 'making sick' means — striking down and devastating; then verses 14-15 explain what **'striking down'** and **'devastating'** will look like.

Yahweh states his judgement in three main clauses, each of which begins with the emphatic *second*-person singular pronoun, **'you'**:[24]

> **'You will eat — and not be satisfied'** (6:14).
> **'You will sow — and will not harvest'** (6:15).

'**You will tread olives — and not anoint yourself**' (6:15).

The first and third of these statements are developed a bit.

Before going on, let me deal with a couple of knotty textual points. One is the second line of verse 14. It speaks of 'your *yeśah* in your insides'. The Hebrew word is only used here; no one can be sure what it means, from ancient versions to modern commentators. Guesses include hunger and dysentery.[25] I have taken the conjunction at the beginning of the clause as adversative (**'but'**) and assumed that something like **'hunger'** fits the context (cf., e.g., NIV, NRSV, NBV). The meaning of the next verb, apparently a causative form from *swg*, means 'to remove' and perhaps 'to put away' or 'carry away'. Others think it is derived from *nāśag*, 'to reach', or 'attain to', and take it in the sense of reaching the point of giving birth (Waltke; cf. NJPS). We cannot be sure. I have taken the former option; they may try to carry away and protect livestock or foodstuffs, but without success, for the enemy will have them.

Yahweh then lays out the form the judgements will take. They focus on a failure of foodstuffs — appropriate for folk who use skimpy ephahs and cheating scales (6:10-11). These judgements come from the covenant curses which Moses had detailed in Deuteronomy 28 (see especially vv. 30-33,38-41). Futility, or frustration, is the common denominator in them. They will eat, but not be satisfied (6:14); they may stash away goods or livestock for safe keeping, but Yahweh will allow the enemy to discover and destroy them (6:14); they will plant grain, but not harvest the crop (6:15). Nor is it just the spring grain crops that let them down (either as a result of a poor crop or of enemy marauding) — their autumn crops (olives, grapes) will not be enjoyed either (6:15).[26] Oh, they will pour their sweat into those olive and grape harvests, but they won't enjoy the result — no skin treatments for one's wife, and no wine for parties to celebrate gathering in the harvest. Futility is the name of the game — like my neighbour who once changed the oil in his vehicle: he drained out the old oil from the crankcase and poured the new oil in, but forgot to replace the drainage plug, and the new oil simply ran out onto the ground. That is the form Yahweh's judgements can take: one invests so much energy and effort and yet gets no return; something — or someone — always messes things up.

6:16
'And the statutes of Omri are observed,
along with all the works of the house of Ahab,
and you have walked in line with their tactics
— in order that I might make you an object of horror
and her residents something to scorn,
and you will bear the disgrace of my people.'

Here the Lord adds another detail that points up how proper his judgement is and depicts the disdain that the surrounding world will have for devastated Judah. The first verb is literally, 'he observes', with a third-person singular subject. I take this verb impersonally ('one observes') and so translate it as an English passive (**'statutes … are observed'**). I do not think, as some do, that the third-person singular subject refers to the king. The following verbs (**'have walked'**, **'will bear'**) are second-person plurals, implying that the people in general are the culprits. And Keil shows how well verse 16 caps off the section, for the first half of the verse corresponds to verses 10-12 (offences), and the second half to verses 13-15 (judgements).[27]

So Yahweh complains that there is an ethos like that of **'Omri'** and an atmosphere of **'Ahab'** in Judah. These two kings (spanning approximately 885–853 BC) were arguably the most corrupt in the (probably by now defunct) northern kingdom (1 Kings 16:25,30-33). (The suggestion is that it's not as if Judah is irreligious; she has her 'fathers in the faith' — Omri and Ahab!) One can get a taste of the climate in Ahab's regime at least from 1 Kings 21; it was a time when the powerful simply ran over, crushed and spat out whoever they liked — witness the graves of Naboth and his family and the altered deeds of ownership on his property. Those in Judah who were in a position to do so have bought into the Omri-Ahab tradition: **'you have walked in line with their tactics'**. The policies and schemes that drove Judah's life smelled as though Jezebel had been resurrected before her time and was once more in charge.

In the second half of this verse Yahweh represents Judah as deliberately goading him to bring ruin on them. 'You have walked,' he says, in this Omri-Ahab rut **'in order that I might make you an object of horror'**. 'The punishment is represented as intentionally brought about by the sinners themselves, to give prominence to the daring with which men lived on in godlessness and unrighteousness.'[28] They have a reckless abandon for horror, scorn and disgrace.

Application

We must see, first, *the wrapping of grace in the warning of judgement* (6:9). 'Give heed to the rod' is both severe and gracious. Calvin picks up on this latter note: 'It is an inestimable privilege for God to warn us of our faults... Thus our Lord sends us threats and exhortations as remedies and as incentives to lead us to repentance.' Hence he says, 'Let us never despise this form of God's grace.'[29] And grace it is, for God is not obligated to warn us. Warning may be the obnoxious side of grace, but it is grace nevertheless. When we hear, 'Give heed to the rod,' it is the judging God seeking to make his judgement unnecessary.

Secondly, especially in verses 10-12, we see *the 'messiness' of God in the exposure of wrong*. In this I am picking up on Leslie Allen's remark that this God 'is no Olympian, remote from everyday living'. Rather, 'The eyes of Yahweh are in every place, keeping watch on the evil and the good' (Prov. 15:3). And he is there in the banter and dust and hollering of the farmers' market, seeing every dishonest trader who pulls off his sharp deal. But Yahweh calls it wickedness, not business; violence, not ambition; deceit, not advertising.

A word of caution: In our contemporary setting I suppose these verses conjure up images of the fat cats of business or industry or banking — and sometimes rightly so. But don't forget that government is the biggest business and seldom hesitates (despite the rhetoric) to milk its subjects. I do not refer merely to the most obviously oppressive regimes, like Robert Mugabe's, which is currently driving poor Zimbabwe into the pit. I mean governments of Western democracies who secure funds via taxation (some of which is legitimate), but squander those 'earnings' by waste and graft and corruption — and so steal more through ever higher, more extensive taxes.

Finally, one should note *the form of judgement in the experience of futility* (6:13-15). Yahweh's judgement may come not via a blazing inferno, but through a whimpering disappointment. In these verses Yahweh naturally depicts how these 'futility curses' affect an agricultural society. But who cannot see that the same form of judgement can take place in an industrial society under a slightly different guise? Labour disputes that halt productivity; transportation workers' strikes that bring a nation to a standstill; rising inflation that eats up earnings (making more, accumulating less); military power that cannot seem to win wars. And individuals continually meet with God's 'futility' judgements — though they may not recognize them. 'There is an evil that I have seen under the sun, and it lies heavy on mankind: a man to whom God gives wealth, possessions, and honour, so that he lacks nothing of all that he desires, yet God does not give him power to enjoy them, but a stranger enjoys them' (Eccles. 6:1-2, ESV). Marvin Olasky tells of Henry R. Rouse, whose men struck oil during the 'black gold' days in the USA. Rouse so enjoyed watching his gusher that he lit a cigar to celebrate. But a spark suddenly set the pooled oil on fire — he dashed through the flames and fell near the edge of the blaze, severely burned. His friends dragged him out. He remained conscious long enough to dictate his will.[30] We must be alert. God's judgement may not appear in a massive outburst of fury, but in a quiet experience of futility.

Sometimes you just want to cry
(Micah 7:1-7)

When in 1566 Queen Mary seemed to be in the ascendancy and he had to leave Edinburgh for the west, John Knox prayed: 'Lord Jesus, receive my spirit, and put an end at Thy good pleasure to this my miserable life, for justice and truth are not to be found among the children of men.'[31] It's hard to avoid despair when your nation and the cause of Christ in it seem to be going to wreck and ruin. One gets a whiff of the same in Micah's lament here in 7:1-7. I doubt that we can date the text specifically, but it was probably some time before 700 BC. The prophet knows that Yahweh's judgement both must come and is coming on Judah (6:9-15), and that Judah is walking in lockstep behind Israel into the sewer-line of history (6:16).

We can too easily detach ourselves from this, as if it's not much skin off our noses at this point. But what happens to the church in this scenario? It's called the 'remnant'. How will the Lord's true people get on until — and when — judgement comes crashing down on their nation? Micah faces that in this passage; he depicts the trouble of having to live in a godless society and of facing the judgement that is coming on that society. The passage poses the question: 'What is it like for a remnant believer living in a society and nation that are going to pot?' And part of the prophet's answer is: 'Sometimes you just want to cry.'

7:1-2a
Woe to me!
For I have become like the gatherings of summer fruit,
   like the gleanings of the grape harvest —
there's not a cluster to eat,
   no early fig that my soul craves.
Covenant man has perished from the land,
and there is no one upright among men...

This comes out in his opening exclamation: **'Woe to me!'** The same particle occurs elsewhere only in Job 10:15, but the tone is similar to some of the 'psalms of lament' (Allen points to Ps. 5; 13; 31, for example). Here he grieves over his *spiritual isolation.* When he says, **'I have become like...'**, he means that his situation is like what he portrays in his analogy. Micah's word picture falls into an ABB¹A¹ pattern:

A   Like the gatherings of summer fruit
    B   like the gleanings of the grape harvest
    B¹ not a cluster to eat
A¹ no early fig.

The **'cluster'** in B¹ is what is missing in the **'grape harvest'** of B, while the lack of an **'early fig'** in A¹ belongs to the category of **'summer fruit'** in A.[32] The first crop of figs ripens in June, the second in August.[33] The first ripe fig had a sort of emotional appeal — here it was, after a long season of abstinence from figs! Leslie Allen compares it to the appeal of the first strawberries of the season to an Englishman. Grape harvest would come round about September, but in Micah's scenario there are no clusters left. Of course, according to the Torah, there *should* have been something left — produce was not to be picked bare, but some was to be left for the poor and widows (Lev. 19:9-10; Deut. 24:19-21). But if **'gleanings'** refers to the second going-over of field or vineyard (as Andersen

and Freedman suggest), then there is nothing left. All
has been picked clean.

In the opening lines of verse 2 Micah drops the
analogy and explains his picture. He is not worried
over the absence of delectable fruit, but over the disappearance of godly people. **'Covenant man'** is my
rendering of *ḥasîd;* the term is linked to *ḥesed,* occurring in 6:8, where it describes the man who 'loves
mercy'.[34] Alec Motyer gathers up the nuances of the
term when he says it refers to 'those whom God loves
with an unchanging love and who love him back'.[35]
Part of that 'loving him back' consists in loving to
show mercy to others (cf. 6:8). So there is no *ḥasîd*
man and, similarly, no **'upright'** (*yāšār*) man — i.e., no
one who conforms his life to the 'straight' standard of
Yahweh's covenant law (cf. Exod. 15:26). The prophet
means that all the people who act as salt and light
(Matt. 5:13-16) are gone. What is there to retard the
rot? And, besides, that means it's very lonely for the
Lord's servant.

7:2b-4a

... All of them lie in ambush to shed blood;
each one hunts down his brother with a net.
As for evil, both hands do it so well;
the official, along with the judge, keeps demanding a pay-off,
and the great one keeps talking of what *he* wants,
and so they weave it together.
The best of them is like a brier bush,
the most upright a thorn hedge...

Micah now details the *social peril.* His sketch resem-
bles Psalm 12:1-2,7-8. Times are simply dangerous
and a lot of the trouble comes via the government
(7:3).[36] Never underestimate what government can do
(see, e.g., 1 Kings 21; Dan. 3).

We might call the latter part of verse 2 the
prophet's general summary of the trouble. He begins

with an emphatic **'all of them'** (*kullām*), which contrasts with the singulars in the first part of the verse; there was not a *ḥasîd*-man or an upright man left, but 'all of them' are bent on violence. This social peril then is, first, total ('all of them'); second, intentional (**'lie in ambush'**); third, violent (**'to shed blood'**); fourth, energetic (**'each one hunts down'**); and, fifth, treacherous (**'hunts ... his brother'**). But can it really be this bleak? Is the picture overdrawn? Micah seems to specify who 'all of them' are in verse 3 — government bureaucrats and judges and people with 'clout'.

The first line of verse 3 is tough to translate. Literally, it reads, 'Upon [or, 'about'] the evil both hands to do well.' He apparently means that both hands are occupied with evil and seek to carry it out in an 'excellent' (i.e., successful) way.[37] He is being sarcastic, indicating what gusto and enthusiasm these officials have for executing their dastardly schemes.

The prophet then specifies **'the official'**; the word is *śar* and denotes rulers and leaders of varied rank under the king.[38] With the official he links **'the judge'** — and these two are in cahoots in **'demanding a payoff'**. **'Demanding'** (*šō'ēl*) is a participle and indicates continuous, ongoing action. Requiring bribes is regular procedure.

Then there is **'the great one'**. Waltke thinks the term refers to the king or his representative. At any rate, he is one who has the influence to 'get things fixed' as he likes. Micah says the great one, literally, 'keeps talking about the desire of his soul'. The word for 'desire' (*hawwâ*) is always used in a bad sense.[39] At the end of the third line of verse 3, Micah has the third-person masculine singular pronoun (*hû'*). It's a bit tricky to know just how to take this, but the prophet seems to be underscoring the 'weightiness' of this 'great one', and so I have tried to catch the sense in a somewhat free rendering: **'the great one keeps talking of what *he* wants'**.

All these power-players **'weave it together'** — they 'co-operate' on all levels and so neuter their opposition, drop them into the social rubbish skip, and have their own way.[40] There is nothing theoretical about this in Micah's time, or ours. I have read that 'public security' officials entered the residence of a Chinese evangelist and beat one of his sons with iron bars for almost half an hour. His mother called an ambulance, but the receptionist told the mother that a higher government authority had given her instructions not to dispatch an ambulance for her son. They 'weave it together'. Ask Christians in Egypt or in India what happens when Muslim men kidnap a Christian girl, or when Hindu extremists attack and maul an assembly of worshipping Christians. Strangely enough, the police merely stand by and / or they never seem to get to the bottom of it. So 'they weave it together'.

Micah's verbal gun is still loaded with sarcasm. He says that the **'best'** of these high-ranking lowlifes is like **'a brier bush'**, the **'most upright'** is a **'thorn hedge'** (7:4).[41] In short, the finest of these thugs can rip you to shreds.

7:4b
… the day of your watchmen —
   the day of your punishment — has come;
now will be their panic time.

Here the prophet announces *national ruin*. **'Your watchmen'** refers to the prophets who warn of judgement (for the idea, see Hosea 9:8; Jer. 6:17; Ezek. 3:17; 33:7; Hab. 2:1). The **'day'** they threatened has arrived. That day is identified as **'your punishment'**; literally, it is your 'visitation', but in this context it means a divine visit for disaster, not deliverance. He then switches — we should be used to it by now — to a third-person pronoun: **'now will**

be their panic time'.[42] I take **'your'** and **'their'** to refer to the same people; the reference could be primarily to the corrupt politicians in verse 3, or even to the guilty nation in general. However, whatever trouble comes upon the whole nation will engulf the believing remnant as well. There is no exemption capsule that believers can enter and get transported to safety. Texts like this implicitly raise the question of what happens to the faithful remnant in such times.

7:5-6
Don't put any faith in a companion;
don't trust in a friend;
guard the doors of your mouth
    from the one who sleeps with you;
for son is going to count [his] father a fool;
daughter rises up against her mother,
daughter-in-law against her mother-in-law
— a man's enemies are the men in his own house!

The prophet now laments a fourth sign of his times: *relational infidelity*.[43] It has (and will) become so dangerous that you cannot trust those closest to you. The danger does not merely lie 'out there' (7:2-4) but 'in here'. A believer in Judah faces both social peril and domestic treachery. The verb forms in the first two lines of verse 5 (**'Don't put any faith'**; **'don't trust'**) are second-person plurals; the group he warns could be the people at large, or, perhaps especially, the members of the believing remnant.

Micah projects an increasing level of both intimacy and disappointment in verse 5. He speaks of a **'companion'** (*rēa'*), then of a (close) **'friend'** (*'allûp*), and finally of the spouse who shares one's bed.[44] One dare not trust any of them. Leslie Allen puts it well:

The prophet gradually penetrates to the centre of these inner circles of familiarity: friend–best friend–wife. A man is now forced to go against his nature, retiring within himself and keeping his own counsel, if he is not to face betrayal. His nearest and dearest cannot be relied on to keep faith with the secrets of his heart. Intimacy is no guarantee of fidelity.[45]

The **'for'** in the opening line of verse 6 introduces the reason for such mandated mistrust. As there was a triple scale of intimacy in verse 5, so the prophet highlights three ruined relationships in verse 6 (son versus father; daughter versus mother; daughter-in-law versus mother-in-law). In the last line Micah moves from samples to principle: 'A man's accusers are the men [or women] in his own house!' And readers are meant not merely to understand the description, but to feel the tragedy.

Jesus picks up verse 6 in his own teaching. He shows us that allegiance to him may be tragic and heart-rending (Matt. 10:35-36; Luke 12:52-53), precisely because he brings division rather than cohesion. Being in Christ can transform relationships; it can also destroy them. And this is not some 'end-time' affair — in Mark 13:12-13 Jesus is still describing what will be characteristic of the present age. So faithfulness to Christ may make family relationships worse! Those who loved you most may hate you more. Legions of believers have found it so — including Christian Gerson, the Jewish-German pawnbroker who in 1600 begins to read a New Testament a customer had pawned, comes to believe in Jesus and hears his wife insist that he leave her and their two sons; and, far more recently, Fatima Al-Mutairi in Saudi Arabia, killed by her own brother, a Muslim cleric, because she had confessed faith in Christ.[46]

7:7
But I, I will look eagerly for Yahweh;
I will wait for the God of my salvation;
my God will hear me.

At the beginning of this section I mentioned that
sometimes believers may simply want to cry over
conditions in their land. That was the case with Micah. That is how he began: 'Woe to me!' But he does
more. Here in verse 7 the prophet not only cries over
ruin but confesses his faith in the midst of that ruin.
He not only bemoans but believes, not only laments
but looks to Yahweh.

Perhaps the best way to get a handle on this verse
is to pick apart what it shows about the prophet's
faith.

In the first place, *faith rises in antithesis*: **'But I, I
will look...'** The first-person pronoun is emphatic,
and I have tried to capture that by repeating it in
translation. The contrast (**'But I'**) shows that Micah
takes his stand in opposition to all that is covered in
verses 1-6. This is often what faith must do — stand
against and stand alone. You persevere and take your
stand in spite of the ruin on its way and in spite of the
isolation you may experience. You will stay by Yahweh
even if your own household (7:5-6) does not.

Secondly, *faith endures in anticipation*: **'I will look
eagerly for Yahweh; I will wait for the God of my
salvation.'** **'Look eagerly'** is from the same root (*sph*)
as 'watchmen' in verse 4. 'Look eagerly' and **'wait for'**
are 'faith' verbs.[47] Mackay captures their import when
he says, 'Waiting is an expression of personal inability
to bring about progress in the situation, and an
expression of God's ability to hear and help.'[48] To look
and wait for Yahweh means one is both desperate and
expectant, for it means I believe *only* Yahweh can
help, but also that Yahweh *will* help. The time is not
immediate — one must 'wait'; but Yahweh will take

care of this at some point in the future. Such looking and waiting is not a cop-out, but a clear-headed realization that Yahweh alone is adequate to handle the matter.

Thirdly, *faith rests in assurance*: **'my God will hear me'**. He is sure his plea will not fall on deaf ears. He speaks of **'Yahweh'**, then of the **'God of my salvation'**, and now of **'my God'**. Yahweh is not a distant God, nor some official, token national deity, but a personal God who will save — the very kind of God one needs for living in a hostile environment in a nation that is plunging to judgement. Micah doesn't have a disaster-response plan; he doesn't form a remnant political caucus; all his hope rests on Yahweh, his Saviour who hears him.

Application

This passage presses two considerations upon us: first, what you may face (7:1-6); and, secondly where you must stand (7:7). We can only reflect on the first one here.

Micah describes his 'world' — its loneliness (7:1-2), its danger and injustice (7:2-4), the fact that it's wobbling on the edge of judgement (7:4), the betrayal that it brings (7:5-6). Yet there is a strain of teaching in Christian circles that says God would never put his servant in such a dreadful situation, that it's not God's will for his children to suffer under such circumstances. Micah would say that is hogwash. And so does the New Testament. Note the finely balanced teaching in Hebrews 11:32-40, where we hear the whole truth about the Christian life. The writer ticks off the previous triumphs of faith: for example, stifling lions, quenching fire, escaping death, chasing armies, enjoying resurrections. Then, in the middle of verse 35, he abruptly cites the rest of the evidence: 'some were tortured', and there were chains and mockings and imprisonments; 'they were stoned, they were sawn in two'; some ended up with nothing to wear but the skins of sheep and goats, nowhere but mountains and deserts to frequent, nothing but caves and holes in the ground for shelter. Lest someone spout nonsense about a lack of faith, the writer adds that 'these all' — desert-wanderers as well as lion-stoppers — 'received approval through faith' (Heb. 11:39).

William Shirer, in *The Nightmare Years*, described the effect of the first British bombs that fell on Berlin during the night of 25 August 1940. They didn't actually do much damage. No one was killed. But they made a huge dent in German morale. This was the first time bombs had ever fallen on Berlin. Shirer said Berliners were stunned. They didn't think it could happen. Hermann Goering had assured them it couldn't. Shirer said that one had to see the Berliners' faces the next day to sense their disillusionment.

There is no reason for God's remnant to live under illusions. Micah has clearly portrayed the circumstances that remnant believers may face. These circumstances are not the defeat of God's design, but the context in which he calls us to watch and wait for the God of our salvation.

Will the church go belly-up?
(Micah 7:8-17)

Here at 7:8 we are at the 'hinge' of the third section of
Micah's book (see the introduction, pp. 14-15). The
third section covers 6:1 – 7:20; the first part focuses
on judgement (6:1 – 7:7), the second on hope (7:8-20).
So at 7:8 we enter the portion bringing a message of
hope, or grace. That is the broad breakdown in terms
of form. However, to follow the main emphases of
chapters 6 – 7 we might divide it into three segments:
first, the presentation of Yahweh's case (6:1-16);
second, the lamentation of Yahweh's prophet (7:1-7);
and, third, the endurance of Yahweh's remnant
(7:8-20).

Within 7:8-17 there are three sections: verses 8-10,
11-13 and 14-17. Leslie Allen calls the first a psalm of
confidence, the second an oracle of salvation and the
third a prayer of supplication.[49] Preferred dates and
historical setting for this material run the gamut; I
think it likely that Micah is anticipating the scourge
under Babylon and beyond (he was aware of that,
according to 4:9-10, which I accept as authentic).[50]

Why does it all matter? What is the *concern* that
underlies this text? Well, we have heard the accusation of 6:1-8 and have followed the judgement
mapped out in 6:9-16 — and then read of the desperate straits of the remnant in, for example, 7:2. What,
we might think, will we hear next? Will chapter 7 close
out with a prophecy about entering an age of pure
paganism? Will the church go belly-up? Was the

intention of having a faithful people in this nasty
world a really fine idea, but a bit much for even God to
hope for? Micah will have none of it. He avows that,
though the fortunes of Judah look bleak, even though
by God's appointment she will be put through the
Babylonian wringer, still the church / remnant will *not*
go belly up, for several good reasons. But more on
those later.

7:8-10

Do not rejoice over me, my enemy;
when I fall, I shall rise again;
when I sit in darkness,
    Yahweh will be a light to me.
I will bear Yahweh's rage,
for I have sinned against him,
until he takes up my case
and brings about justice for me;
he will bring me forth to the light;
I will look on his righteousness.
And may my enemy see
and may shame cover her
— the one who keeps saying to me,
    'Where is he — Yahweh your God?'
My eyes will see her —
    Now she will become something to be trampled,
    like street mud.

These verses are a warning to the enemies of God's
people: they must not celebrate Judah's disaster, for
they themselves will eat the mud of the streets. In
verse 8 the prophet is speaking for the believing
remnant, so in declaring his faith he declares the faith
of the remnant. When he speaks of falling and sitting
in darkness, he is envisaging the time when the
disaster foretold in 6:16 has come to pass, most likely
'what Jerusalem was to suffer at the hands of the
Babylonians'.[51] Darkness can be paralleled with

disaster (Isa. 45:7), and being or sitting in darkness is associated with confinement and imprisonment (Ps. 107:10; Isa. 42:7; 49:9). Note that Micah not only says, **'I shall rise again'**, but that *even while* he sits in darkness, **'Yahweh will be a light to me.'** Yahweh not only **'will bring me forth to the light'** (7:9), but is himself my light in the midst of the darkness.

The first two lines of verse 9 clearly reveal that we are dealing here with the *believing* remnant, for unbelief never manifests such sensitivity to sin (**'for I have sinned against him'**) and willingness to endure the judgement that must be inflicted because of it (**'I will bear Yahweh's rage'**).[52] The remnant knows it will not be miraculously exempt from the coming scourge, but is willing to acknowledge its own guilt as a part of a whole unfaithful people. Only believing hearts are soft like this.

Two terms, at opposite poles, wrap around verse 9 — Yahweh's **'rage'** (*za'ap*) and his **'righteousness'** (*ṣedāqâ*). The former the prophet endures; the latter he anticipates. I take **'righteousness'** here as meaning 'vindication', in view of the 'legal' terminology in the verse. That terminology includes the hope that Yahweh **'takes up my case'** (the verb is *rîb* plus cognate direct object; see the same pattern in Ps. 43:1, 'plead my case') and **'brings about justice for me'** (literally, 'he shall accomplish my justice'; see Ps. 9:4-5).[53] One sees both sides of Yahweh's judgement in this verse: it is a scourge that must be endured, and it is a hope to be longed for. Of the former Waltke says it is both just (**'for I have sinned against him'**) and temporary (**'until ...'**).[54] But after that 'until' the remnant can expect Yahweh to put things right for them. The assumption is probably that injustice will be inflicted upon them by those who will decimate them (cf., e.g., Isa. 47:6) and in his time Yahweh will take up the cudgels for his people by bringing judgement down on those who had been instruments of his judgement on his own people. In that sense, having God as judge is good news; it's why in Psalm 96 the world goes ecstatic; it knows a time is coming when the Judge will put everything to rights.[55]

Most translations take the first two verbs of verse 10 as indicatives. I think they are jussives — i.e., ones that should be translated as subjunctives in English; hence, **'may my enemy see'**, **'may shame cover her'**.[56] This the remnant anticipates. They do so because of the enemy's mockery not only of Zion, but of Yahweh. The enemy **'keeps saying'** (participle, indicating repeated action), **'Where is he — Yahweh your God?'** The **'your'** in **'your God'** is feminine, alluding to Lady Zion.[57] This is the mockery that galled the Lord's servant in Psalm 42:3,10. It implies the helplessness of Yahweh, insinuates he is useless to deliver. It's the kind of thing behind the mockery of Psalm 137:3: 'Sing us something from a Zion song!' It was religious ridicule, especially of Yahweh, who is depicted as powerless to defend and protect his people. The implied answer to the gibe, 'Where is he?' is: 'He's nowhere to be found! It's pretty useless to have a god like that!'

But all this will be reversed. The remnant will see the enemy swallow her scorn and sneers. The verb here is indicative (**'will see'**), partly because the subject (**'my eyes'**) is in emphatic position before the verb; hence a contrary, assertive statement is being made: **'*My eyes* will see her.'**[58] The **'her'** is **'my enemy'** (7:10), since 'enemy' is feminine.[59] It's the typical trend: those who deride Yahweh eat street dirt. So Calvin says in his customary way, 'We now understand the design of the Prophet — that he wished to arm us ... against the taunts of the ungodly.'[60] In these verses then, Micah shows us the remnant in the darkness (7:8) and after the darkness (7:9), when at last they see Yahweh's **'righteousness'** carried out against those who despise them (7:10).

7:11-13
A day for the building of your walls!
On that day the boundary will be far off.
On that day *to you* they will come
   from Assyria and the cities of Egypt,
   and from Egypt all the way to the River,
   from sea to sea and mountain to mountain.
And the earth shall become a waste
   because of its residents,
   because of the fruit of their deeds.

Here Micah speaks of the light beyond the darkness.[61] In spite of some tricky details, especially in verses 11-12, the general picture is clear: there will be, first, restoration (7:11); second, additions (7:12); and, third, destruction (7:13). Two elements are positive; one is negative.

In verse 11 Micah hails a day beyond the time of Yahweh's rage (7:9) and calls it **'a day for the building of your walls'**. The word *gādēr* does not refer to a city or fortress wall (*ḥômâ* would be the usual term for that), but to a wall built of stones, often without mortar, which encloses vineyards (Isa. 5:5; Ps. 80:12; cf. Num. 22:24) or sheep-pens (the feminine cognate, in Num. 32:16,24,36), or even a wall in Ezekiel's temple (Ezek. 42:7,10,12). It is not used for a high, protective city wall.[62] I take Micah to be speaking figuratively of restoration, of life being what it should be in an ordered land, with, for example, vineyards and sheep-pens properly constructed, in much the same way that Jeremiah spoke of restored life as once more featuring normal wedding celebrations (Jer. 33:10-11; cf. Jer. 7:34; 16:9; 25:10).

Another feature of that day is that **'the boundary will be far off'** (7:11). **'Boundary'** is the word *ḥōq*. The word refers to what is prescribed, set, or decreed, and so regularly means 'a decree', 'edict', or 'statute', often one laid down by God.[63] Some insist that here it must

mean a law or statute, perhaps God's statute requiring Israel's separation from the nations, which would
be lifted (Keil, Kleinert), or the 'edict' of Babylon,
which, by God's mercy, will no longer hold sway over
Israel (Calvin). It is a disputed point. In view of the
geographical expansion described in verse 12, I have
taken the term figuratively as 'boundary' (Job 14:5,13;
26:10; 38:10; Jer. 5:22).

Verse 12 begins with another reference to this
coming **'day'** — there were two in verse 11, and now
'on that day' introduces verse 12. If my view of this
verse is correct, this 'day' seems to be a parallel to the
future time depicted in 4:1-2.

However, the next clause is a poser: 'and to you
[emphatic] he [or "it"] will come'. The **'you'** is usually
taken as Zion or the people of God; if that were the
case, the 'you' would normally be feminine (as in verse
11), but here it is masculine. Some would say it
makes little difference, because (as Waltke comments)
switching between genders is common in poetry, and
so it still refers to Lady Zion. However, the use of the
masculine might indicate that Micah is briefly addressing Yahweh. In that case the sense would be: as
well as Yahweh's people knowing restoration (7:11),
other nations will come not merely to Zion, but to
Yahweh (7:12). The singular verb form ('he [or "it"] will
come') is still a conundrum. I have taken it in an
impersonal sense ('one will come'), with the pronoun
fleshed out by the following references to people from
Assyria and Egypt, and so have translated it as a
plural (**'they will come'**).

But who is to come **'from Assyria and the cities of
Egypt'**? Some think they are exiles returning from
later captivity, but in that case, as Keil points out, one
would expect the verb to be 'return' (a form of *šûb*)
rather than **'come'** (*bô'*).[64] So the last three lines of the
verse seem to depict, in an ascending, expanding
form, the coming of the Gentiles to Yahweh and / or

his people. They come from the then-current scourge
of Judah, Assyria, and from the cities of their ancient
oppressor, Egypt.[65] Then the prophet opens up the
field to include every nook and corner of the world —
they come from Egypt and **'all the way to the River'**
(the Euphrates) and then, literally, 'all the way to the
sea from the sea and to the mountain of the mountain'. The literal expression is a bit awkward, but it's
the prophet's way of saying, 'from all the lands and
provinces of the earth'.[66]

Verse 13 presents the reverse side of verse 12. Of
course, *'ereṣ* can be 'land' (NJPS) or **'earth'**, but in
view of the scope of verse 12 we should take the word
in its universal sense. Because of the sin and wickedness of the earth's residents (I take both prepositions,
'al and *min*, in the first part of verse 13 in a causal
sense), Yahweh will bring devastation on it (see the
teaching of Isaiah 24). I don't think we should worry
ourselves too much about how both salvation (7:12)
and devastation (7:13) will come about for the nations.
What we need to see is that here, as elsewhere in the
prophets, we find the double edge of Yahweh's truth:
some among the nations will come to a saving submission (7:12) and others will endure a scourging
judgement. (One might say that the former is as
undeserved as the latter is deserved.) Verse 13 is
solemn. There is always this corollary of the genuine
gospel: if 'nations shall come to your light' (Isa. 60:3),
there are others who prefer the outer darkness; if
there are those who 'come' (here in 7:12), there is
nevertheless an 'outside' (Rev. 22:15).

7:14-17
Shepherd your people with your rod,
    the flock you possess,
        dwelling by themselves in a forest,
            in the middle of a garden land.
Let them graze in Bashan and Gilead

as in days of long ago.
'As in the days when you came out from the land of Egypt
   I will show him wonders.'
Let nations see
and let them be ashamed of all their might.
Let them put hand over mouth,
let their ears be deaf;
let them lick dust like the serpent,
   like the crawling things of earth;
let them come shaking from their fortifications.
To Yahweh our God let them come in dread
and let them be afraid of you.

Let's first trace the pattern of these verses. Verse 14 is
a prayer, the prophet speaking for the believing remnant. Verse 15, as it stands, is a one-line assurance
given by Yahweh (note the switch to the first person: **'I
will show him wonders'**).[67] Then verses 16-17 are
either Micah's prophecy of the pagan nations' demise
(using indicative verbs, e.g., 'Nations will see and be
ashamed,' as in NASB, ESV, NIV, NRSV), or a continuation of Micah's prayer picked up from verse 14
(featuring verbs taken as jussives, e.g., **'let nations
see and let them be ashamed'**, as in NJPS). I think
this second option is preferable and I have translated
the verbs of verses 16-17 accordingly.[68] The text then
falls out like this:

Prayer for Yahweh's flock (7:14)
   Assurance from Yahweh's promise (7:15)
Prayer for the nations' submission (7:16-17)

This teaches us that we ought to *wrap* our prayers
around promises; in verses 16-17, it seems, the
prophet is pleading on the basis of verse 15. With this
sketch in mind, let us wade through the details of the
text.

Micah asks Yahweh to **'shepherd your people ... the flock you possess'** (7:14). This certainly points to remnant Israel (cf. Waltke); however, in view of verse 12, it may also include the 'Assyrian' and 'Egyptian' types who will come in faith and worship to Yahweh. **'Your people'**, given the context, may hint that the olive tree (see Rom. 11) sports more than just Israelite branches.

In the rest of verse 14 Micah asks that Yahweh would provide abundantly for his flock. Echoing Balaam's description, he describes them as **'dwelling by themselves'** (see Num. 23:9). Some think that **'in a forest'** refers to overgrown scrubland, and so is a picture of distress.[69] But I doubt it. 'Forest' or 'forest land' (*ya'ar*) does not regularly indicate overgrown scrubland.[70] It occurs with **'garden land'** (*karmel*), as it does here, in descriptions of lavish fertility, sometimes indicating a step up from the level described as *karmel* (see Isa. 10:18; 29:17; 32:15).[71] And Numbers 32 helps us with the last line of verse 14; there the tribes of Reuben, Gad and half-Manasseh salivated over Bashan and Gilead, east of the Jordan, precisely because the regions were ideally suited for livestock.

As Keil pointed out, we should connect Micah's prayer in this verse with the promise of 5:4.[72] There we were told that the future Bethlehem-originating ruler over Israel (5:2) 'shall stand and act as shepherd in the strength of Yahweh ... and they shall dwell securely'. Here in 7:14 the prophet prays that the promise of 5:4 might come to pass, that the messianic shepherd would come and prove to be the protection (**'with your rod'**) and provision (**'let them graze'**) of his people.

The heart of verses 14-17, however, is the promise of verse 15.[73] The **'wonders'** (*niplā'ôt*) of Egypt are the plagues, the deliverance at the sea and provision in the wilderness (Exod. 3:20; Judg. 6:13; Ps. 78:32; 106:7,22). In this one-liner Yahweh assures his people that when he restores them, he will do so in a way that displays all the flair and fury of the Exodus events. Marvellous deeds of Yahweh's outstretched arm will mark Israel's final restoration, as they did their initial salvation. It will not be a time for slow, gradual, subtle, low-key changes, but for explosive events and dramatic deeds — shades of the original fireworks.

In verses 16-17 Micah continues his prayer (see comments at the beginning of this section) in response to Yahweh's word in verse 15.[74]

He prays for the nations' *frustration* (7:16). **'Ashamed of all their might'** is, literally, 'ashamed *from* all their might' — that is, 'without', or 'deprived of', their might (see NIV), and so they cannot use their power to disrupt the security of Yahweh's restored people.

He prays for their *consternation* (7:16). Clapping one's hand over one's mouth signals shock and wonder (cf. Job 21:5; 29:9; 40:4). When he asks that their ears should become deaf, he pictures how upset the nations are over the reversal of Israel's fortunes. 'The news that reaches them is such that they will refuse to listen to it.'[75] It drives them crazy; they don't want to hear it.

And he prays for their *humiliation* (7:17); to **'lick dust'**, like a serpent or crawling things, is a picture of utter defeat and subjugation (see Ps. 72:9; Isa. 49:23; cf. Gen. 3:14).

Then he asks for their *intimidation* (7:17). Micah uses three verbs here which convey the sense of 'fear'; the first two (*rāgaz* and *pāḥad*) are quite vivid, referring to shaking and trembling in dread. **'To Yahweh our God'** is emphatic in the Hebrew text since it is placed before the verb *pāḥad* (my translation reflects this).[76] This is not the 'fear' of repentance or faith.[77] It is terror without trust, fright without faith. The nations face an either / or situation: they can come to Yahweh in

submission (7:11-12), or else they will come in panic
(7:16-17).

Application

We come back to an earlier question: Will the church go belly-up
and become extinct? No, Micah says, for three reasons.

First, because *God's anger is passing* (7:8-10). In the darkness, there is light and consolation (7:8), and after the darkness,
restoration and vindication (7:9-10). Yahweh's rage, though just,
doesn't go on and on. We have no indication here *why* his rage
turns away; we are only told that it will. No wonder we have hope
even in the 'darkness' (cf. Lam. 3:31-32; Ps. 103:9-10; Isa.
54:7-8). You may know acutely how you need such a God: you
make a wreck of your life, a right royal mess of things, and it's
clearly your own fault; you turned your back on, and shut your ears
to, all godly counsel from others, silenced the voice of your own
conscience, and now simply have to endure the ravages of your
own rebelliousness and his chastisement. You have to say, 'I will
bear Yahweh's rage — for I have sinned against him' (7:9). But if
you come to say that, you find, strangely, that you can also say,
'When I sit in darkness, Yahweh will be a light to me' (7:8).[78]

But the remnant will also not go extinct because *God's people
will be multiplied* (7:11-13). John Tyler, tenth US president, had
an embattled presidency but an extensive progeny. He had eight
children by his first wife Letitia; after she died, he married Julia,
thirty years younger than he was, by whom he fathered seven
more. Tyler himself was born when George Washington was
president and his youngest daughter, born when Tyler was
seventy, died during Harry Truman's tenure. Just the immediate
family covered thirty presidents and over 150 years.[79] Then think
of all the descendants. How could such a brood go extinct? There
were so many! That is the 'argument' of verses 11-12. Yahweh
will begin by restoring his battered people (7:11) and will also
enlarge the circle of the redeemed by drawing in those from
enemy nations (7:12). Even those with Assyrian and Egyptian
passports will be coming to Yahweh (see Isa. 19:16-25). The

programme of Genesis 12:3 will kick in on a grand scale. We see that saving scheme at work throughout the Scriptures, not least in the conversion of Cornelius, for example, in Acts 10 and in the work of the Antioch evangelists in Acts 11:20-21. But, whether with vast numbers or by intermittent trickles, people are being added to the Zion remnant. And how can such a people go belly-up when God keeps adding to their numbers?

There's a third reason why God's remnant will not go down the drain: because *God's power is promised* (7:14-17, but especially verse 15). The church cannot be eradicated because, when the time comes, Yahweh will use his 'Egyptian methods', his bare-arm approach. Then his way will no longer be gradual or partial or incremental; rather he will work in a clearly almighty, public, visible, 'ooh-and-ah' kind of way. The time will come when he will switch to the 'without doubt' supernatural proofs of his power (cf. 1 Thess. 4:16-17; 2 Thess. 1:7-10): Parousia, resurrection, judgement. It will be a time, not for another anaemic UN pronouncement, but for the flexing of the muscles and sinews in Jesus' almighty arm. 'I will show him wonders' — overwhelming omnipotence will be the order of the day.

Not much has changed since Micah's day. Vast numbers despise the church and would love to see her wiped away. And God's people themselves are so prone to faithlessness that, left to themselves, they would disappear down a black hole of history. But Micah knows the reasons why that won't happen. Just imagine — what if Micah had lived 700 years later? What if he had heard what Jesus said in Matthew 16:18? 'I will build my church, and the powers of death shall not prevail against it' (RSV). Micah would turn to us and say, 'See? That's what I have been trying to tell you.'

Come, let us adore him!
(Micah 7:18-20)

Jonathan Edwards had ridden out into the woods, on one occasion in 1737, to a place where he might walk and think and pray; it was then, he said, 'I had a view, that for me was extraordinary, of the glory of the Son of God.' He went on: 'The person of Christ appeared ineffably excellent, with an excellency great enough to swallow up all thought and conception.'[80] That is how Micah ends his book. Oh, Micah would not use phrases like 'ineffably excellent', but his **'Who is a God like you?'** amounts to the same thing. The prophet may have found it hard to put thunder and lightning and racing heartbeat into words, but as Micah began his prophecy with the fury of God's wrath (1:2-9), so now he closes it with the fountain of God's mercy (7:18-20) — and he can scarcely contain himself! He is part of a Babylon-bound people (4:10) who will endure Yahweh's judgement, and yet this believing remnant waits for Yahweh (7:7) and knows that God will in grace bring about restoration (7:8-17). And Micah is simply overcome (7:18). He is like the chief of sinners in 1 Timothy 1:12-17, who could not be satisfied with the twice-stated, awe-filled, 'But I received mercy' (vv. 13, 16), and had to break out into doxology to 'the King of ages, immortal, invisible', in verse 17. So here it is as though Micah is saying to us, 'Join me in being thrilled over the God of all grace, and then come, let us adore him!'

7:18

Who is a God like you,
pardoning iniquity
and passing over rebellion
    for the remnant of his inheritance?
He will not hold on to his anger for ever,
because he delights in unfailing love.

Many point out that the prophet's initial exclamation may be a play on his own name. Micah is an abbreviated form of Micaiah, 'Who is like Yahweh?' Mockers say, 'Where is Yahweh?' (7:10), but the prophet asks, 'Who is like Yahweh?'

Yahweh is incomparable primarily and specifically in his pardoning grace: **'Who is a God like you, pardoning iniquity and passing over rebellion...?'** 'Iniquity' is *'awôn*, which refers to the wrong and / or the guilt incurred by it, and sometimes to the punishment inflicted for it (for the latter, cf. Gen. 4:13). The root means 'to bend' or 'twist'; one might think of wrong in the sense of 'wrung' — something that is twisted, distorted, perverse, a wrong deed that comes from a twisted nature. The other term for sin here is *peša'*, often translated 'transgression', but which carries the idea of rebellion or revolt and usually implies a wilful violation.[81]

This God 'pardons' iniquity. The verb form is a participle of *nāśā'*, which means to 'lift up' and/or 'carry'. The verb occurs in that marvellous picture in the Day of Atonement ritual in Leviticus 16:21-22. Aaron the high priest is to press both his hands down on the head of the live goat, then to confess all the iniquities, rebellions and sins of Israel over it, and, by doing so, he 'shall place them on the head of the goat'. A man then leads the goat to the oblivion of the wilderness. 'And the goat shall *carry* upon it all their iniquities' (Lev. 16:22). The burden of the guilt is transferred to another, and that substitute carries it

all away![82] Which shouldn't surprise us — Yahweh
had already said he is a God who *carries away* 'iniquity and rebellion and sin' (Exod. 34:7). As if this
weren't enough, Micah says Yahweh 'passes over
rebellion'. Maybe he might be willing to overlook
mishaps, we think, or slight errors — but rebellion?
It's like saying a government passes over treason. I
know this is supposed to be exegesis, but look at what
we are carrying out an exegesis of! This is not just
grammar — it's grace. Where have you ever heard of a
God like this?

The prophet says Yahweh does this **'for the remnant of his inheritance'**.[83] This is restrictive. Not
every card-carrying Judean will know this forgiveness. There is Israel at large, and then there is remnant Israel (at that time, Micah and his fellow believers in Judah). Even the remnant must be forgiven.
There is no special merit attaching to them that
places them beyond the need of pardon. Indeed, the
remnant contains the only ones who see their need of
it. What makes the remnant the *faithful* remnant
except the fact that they are acutely aware that they
are a *sinful* people? Note the repentant 'we'/'us' in
Isaiah 53:1-6, and observe that in Ezekiel 36:26,31
precisely those who have a new heart and a new spirit
are the ones who 'loathe themselves' for their iniquities and abominations.

In the last two lines of verse 18 Micah switches
from **'you'** to **'he'**, from second person to third person. The NIV irritatingly ignores this and tries to
'improve' the text by keeping the second-person pronouns. It has done a poor job in this section and
should not be followed here.

In these verses we get as close as we will anywhere
to an explanation of Yahweh's pardoning work: **'He
will not hold on to his anger for ever.'** That is a
marvel in itself (cf. Ps. 103:9). But why will he not?
The next line tells us: *'for'*, or **'because he delights in**

unfailing love'. Micah so much as says, 'He won't hold on to his anger because he loves pleasure and he gets pleasure from showing unfailing love' (*ḥesed*).

Verse 18 comes close to tautology. The prophet seems to say Yahweh acts this way (pardoning, etc.) because that is the way he is. We may be guilty, but we are not irrational and we are left asking, 'But why?' And verse 18 will only say, 'Because it is his pleasure.' Micah wants to stagger us with *the miracle of Yahweh's character.*

7:19
He will again show compassion to us;
he will trample down our iniquities,
and you will heave all their sins
    into the depths of the sea.

The grammatical switches continue: the verbs go from third person (**'he will ... show compassion'**, **'he will trample down'**) in the first two lines to second person (**'you will heave'**) in the third; the **'us'** and **'our'** (first-person plurals) of the first half of the verse switch to **'their'** (third-person plural) in the second. But this does not obscure the sense in any way.

The prophet underscores Yahweh's warmth of compassion (**'He will again show compassion to us'**) and then his exercise of power (**'he will trample down ... you will heave'**); one might say that his exercise of power is the *way* he will show compassion.

The verbs are striking. He will **'trample down'** (*kābaš*) our iniquities.[84] *Their power can no longer hold us.* There is not only a pardon, but a punch in the pardon that sets us free. 'He breaks the power of cancelled sin.' Micah is edging us towards Romans 6:6,14; his doctrine provides a needed antidote to that recurring 'Christian despair' which thinks there is no hope of changing some habit, or ceasing some practice, or reversing some pattern of sinful response in a relationship.

But then the prophet exults: **'And you will heave all their sins into the depths of the sea.'** Note what Yahweh is dealing with — sins, and, in the first part of the verse, iniquities. These are what Waltke calls 'countable' plurals, indicating the massive number, the repeated offences. In case we miss it, Micah is a bit more emphatic in this line: **'*all* their sins'**. Here Yahweh throws sins — the whole tonnage — **'into the depths of the sea'**; in other words, he gives them the 'Egyptian treatment'. Micah's language conjures up Exodus 15:4-5,10. Once those Egyptians went down under, Israel never saw them again (Exod. 14:13). If Yahweh does that with his people's sins, then *their guilt can no longer haunt us*.

What a sweeping picture of forgiveness the prophet paints! In the first half of verse 19 he highlights the idea of dominance (God tramples down iniquities), and so addresses the helplessness of his people; in the second half the matter of place (the depth of the sea) is prominent, and thus addresses the fears of his people (i.e., will their guilt 'come back'?). So Micah has hammered home *the power of Yahweh's forgiveness*.

7:20
May you show faithfulness to Jacob
    and unfailing love to Abraham,
which you swore to our fathers
    from days of long ago.

The prophet continues in prayer mode with the second-person address: **'May you show...'** (literally, 'May you give...'). The verb can be translated either as an indicative or a subjunctive (I prefer the latter). Either way the sense is not materially affected.[85] Micah prays that Yahweh will show **'faithfulness'** (*'ĕmet;* some translate it as 'truth', but 'fidelity', or 'faithfulness', catches it better) to Jacob and **'unfailing love'** (*ḥesed*) to Abraham. A reader could conceivably lose patience at this point. He might say, 'Who cares about Jacob and Abraham, two old geezers from long ago and far away? Why should I care if God is loyal to them? Why do we always have to go back to "days of long ago"?' Answer: 'Because God didn't start working when you came on the scene.'

Without apology Micah takes us back to Yahweh's *ancient* promise (**'which you swore to our fathers'**), namely his commitment to show them this *'ĕmet* and *ḥesed*. But what exactly is this firm fidelity promised to Jacob and this sure love granted to Abraham? The short answer is the promise at the centre of the covenant: 'I will be God to you — and to your seed after you' (Gen. 17:7). In having Yahweh as his God Abraham (the recipient in Genesis 17) has all things, for the promise means that Yahweh will be to him all that God would and should and could be. Moreover, it is an indissoluble relationship, for once Yahweh promises to be your God he can never cease being so — and so no condition, not even death, can sever that relationship or fray his hold upon you. Hence implicit in this promise is resurrection from the dead (it has to be!) and life in the land. The promise to Abraham and the other patriarchs is sufficient to show us this, but to hear Jesus' reasoning on it helps immensely (Mark 12:26-27).[86]

But Micah may also want to bring us to Sinai, for he speaks here of **'unfailing love'** and **'faithfulness'** in a context of 'iniquity', 'rebellion' and 'sins' (7:18-19; note too the use of 'unfailing love' [*ḥesed*] in verse 18 in that connection). All this can hardly fail to conjure up Exodus 34:6-7, Yahweh's proclamation of his name, declaring that he is 'rich in *ḥesed* and *'ĕmet*' and 'forgiving [*nāśā'*, see 7:18 here] iniquity, rebellion, and sin'.[87] That was no bit of theoretical theology, for it was the relieving answer to Moses' anguished intercession for a people guilty of apostasy, who preferred bull-worship to waiting on Yahweh (Exod. 32:1-6). By this collage of vocabulary Micah may be wanting to tell us, 'Yahweh is still the same, and part of that sworn commitment to Jacob and Abraham includes the forgiveness of sins.' And so he leaves us clinging to *the fidelity of Yahweh's word.*

Application

The Authorized/King James Version renders the last line of verse 18 as 'He delighteth in mercy.' It was in this form that the text proved a shaft of comfort to John Carment. Dr Carment was a highly esteemed member of the Edinburgh legal profession. One day his pastor, Alexander Whyte, had to consult Carment on a business matter. With the business completed, the old lawyer (for he was above eighty years old) swept the papers and writing materials to the side, and looking straight across the cleared desk, said with deep earnestness, 'Have ye any word for an old sinner?' Dr Whyte was somewhat taken aback at the sudden question, not least because he esteemed Carment as a saint poised for glory. He drew a momentary blank, but then words came to him which he had given to various ones he had visited that very afternoon. So he stammered out, 'He delighteth in mercy' — and left. Next morning Whyte received a letter from Dr Carment which told how he had been passing through a season of deep inward darkness, but that the four words left with him by his friend had sent a flood of light into his soul. It banished the darkness for good — until in a few days he got his glimpse of perfect day.[88]

   That shows the deep comfort of the text, but I can't grasp that very well unless I see the sheer wonder of it: 'He retaineth not his anger for ever, because he delighteth in mercy' (AV). In short, Yahweh's love of showing his unfailing love is simply ingrained in his nature; it is the inerasable way he is. Peggy Noonan tells of Ronald Reagan's last years. Ravaged by Alzheimer's, he didn't speak much, couldn't really converse, wasn't really 'there'. People fed him and made sure that he wasn't up and about without oversight. But even during those days, Ms Noonan reports that this man was 'so hardwired for courtesy' and with regard for others that when he accidentally bumped the arm of the woman who was feeding him he would say with perfect enunciation, 'Oh, I beg your pardon.'[89] Though disease was stripping his mental gears it did not eradicate his courtesy — it was, Noonan says, *just the way he was.* That's where Micah leaves us. Why does Yahweh not hold on to his anger for ever? Because he delights in mercy. But why does he delight in mercy? I don't know — it's simply the way he is. Micah closes his book and imposes on me a conundrum, a revelation and a duty: I cannot explain why Yahweh is this way, but he is, and I can only adore.

Notes

Introductory matters

1. One can follow a typical discussion like this in Georg Fohrer, *Introduction to the Old Testament* (Nashville: Abingdon, 1968), pp.443-7.
2. Work through H. W. Wolff, *Micah: A Commentary* (Minneapolis: Augsburg, 1990), pp.4-5, 13-14, 17-27, and see.
3. Brevard Childs, *Introduction to the Old Testament as Scripture* (Philadelphia: Fortress, 1979), p.431.
4. This breakdown goes back at least to C. F. Keil, *Biblical Commentary on the Old Testament: The Twelve Minor Prophets* (Grand Rapids: Eerdmans, 1967 [first published 1868], 2 vols), vol. 1, pp.422-4; see his fine discussion.
5. David A. Dorsey prefers a chiastic arrangement of Micah's prophecies with 4:1 – 5:15 as the centrepiece (*The Literary Structure of the Old Testament,* Grand Rapids: Baker, 1999, pp.296-300). Cf. also Kevin C. Peacock, 'Who is a God Like You? — Theological Themes in Micah,' *Southwestern Journal of Theology* 46/1 (Fall 2003): 27-47. Sometimes chiastic arrangements look better on paper than when measured against the text.

1. Through judgement to preservation (1:1 – 2:13)

1. My view, of course. Many others would ascribe the heading to later editors. There's no denying that 'editing' was necessary, for what we have in the prophets' books are not 'sermon tapes' (or else segments would be much, much longer) but a literary edition of the prophets' messages, in which we have a written digest of their preaching. See Alec Motyer's perceptive comments in *Look to the Rock* (Leicester: Inter-Varsity, 1996), p.102. There is no reason why Micah himself could not have done his own editing.
2. Cf. Alec Motyer, 'Prophecy, Prophets,' *NBD*, 3rd edition, p.966.
3. In his own home town Micah would probably have been known as 'the son of [whoever his father was]', but he would be called the **'Morashtite'** if he lived somewhere else, like Jerusalem — see

Francis I. Andersen and David Noel Freedman, *Micah*, Anchor Bible (New York: Doubleday, 2000), p.109.

4. See Andersen and Freedman, *Micah*, pp.123-5; E. J. Young, *My Servants the Prophets* (Grand Rapids: Eerdmans, 1952), pp.176-9, 187-8.

5. See Gary N. Knoppers, 'The Historical Study of the Monarchy: Development and Detours,' in *The Face of Old Testament Studies* (Grand Rapids: Baker, 1999), pp.228-30; and Wolff, *Micah*, p.3. See 2 Kings 15 – 19.

6. See J. B. Pritchard, ed., *ANET*, 3rd edition, pp.391-2.

7. John Calvin, *Sermons on the Book of Micah*, trans. & ed. Benjamin Wirt Farley (Phillipsburg, NJ: Presbyterian & Reformed, 2003), p.5.

8. For the rationale for treating 1:2-9 as a distinct entity, see Leslie C. Allen, *The Books of Joel, Obadiah, Jonah and Micah*, New International Commentary on the Old Testament (Grand Rapids: Eerdmans, 1976), pp.268-9, 274, note 47.

9. On the location, see J. Kelso, 'Samaria,' *ZPEB*, vol. 5, p.232; for a clear and concise historical survey of the site, see Michael Avi-Yonah, 'Samaria', in *Archaeology*, Israel Pocket Library (Jerusalem: Keter, 1974), pp.182-5.

10. The verb (**'heave'**) is *nāgar*, which also appears as a participle in 1:4 (where I translated it as water 'rushing' down a slope). In verse 4, when Yahweh appears, all creation turns liquid, as it were, and waters 'heave themselves', while in verse 6, when Yahweh comes to judge Samaria, *he* heaves its stones down the slope.

11. See M. Cogan and H. Tadmor, *II Kings*, Anchor Bible (Double-day, 1988), pp.198-200 and references there.

12. R. E. Tappy, 'Samaria', *Dictionary of the Old Testament: Historical Books* (Downers Grove, IL: Inter-Varsity, 2005), p.861.

13. See J. Klausner, 'John Hyrcanus I', in *The World History of the Jewish People*, vol. 6: *The Hellenistic Age* (Jerusalem: Massada, 1972), pp.217-18; James D. Purvis, 'Samaria (City),' *ABD*, vol. 5, p.919; and Josephus, *Antiquities*, 13, pp.280-81.

14. T. E. McComiskey, 'Micah', *Expositor's Bible Commentary* (Grand Rapids: Zondervan, 1985, 12 vols), vol. 7, p.405.

15. Allen, *The Books of Joel ... and Micah*, p.274.

16. R. K. Harrison, 'Jackal', *ISBE*, vol. 2, p.947. (I have translated the other term in our text, *ya'ănâ*, 'desert owl'; we can't be sure whether it designates an ostrich or some sort of owl; cf. *NIDOTTE*, vol. 2, p.489).

17. Micah's flair for grammatical conundrums appears in verse 9; for information on these see Andersen and Freedman, *Micah*, pp.195-8.

18. Marjory Bonar, ed., *Andrew A. Bonar: Diary and Life* (Edinburgh: Banner of Truth, 1960), p.511.

19. Cf. P. C. Craigie, *Twelve Prophets*, Daily Study Bible (Philadelphia: Westminster, 1985, 2 vols), vol. 2, p.14, for a Scottish analogy.

20. See Carl G. Rasmussen, *Zondervan NIV Atlas of the Bible* (Grand Rapids: Zondervan, 1989), pp.47-8.

21. See comments in Andersen and Freedman, *Micah*, pp.235, 238, 244. It is, by the way, difficult to know how to divide up verses 10-16. Leslie Allen points out that each of verses 13-15 ends (in the Hebrew text) with **'Israel'** (*The Books of Joel ... and Micah*, p.278), so one might take verses 10-12 (a passage which ends with 'Jerusalem') together, then verses 13-15, and finally verse 16 as a tailpiece.

22. See *Dictionary of the Old Testament: Historical Books*, p.305 (article by Ortiz); and G. A. Turner, *Historical Geography of the Holy Land* (Grand Rapids: Baker, 1973), pp.176-81.

23. See Bruce K. Waltke, 'Micah', in *The Minor Prophets* (Grand Rapids: Baker, 1993, 3 vols), vol. 2, pp.628-9.

24. Cf. Waltke, 'Micah', p.628; *NIDOTTE*, vol. 1, pp.486-7. K. L. Barker suggests 'house of protection' — see K. L. Barker and Waylon Bailey, *Micah, Nahum, Habakkuk, Zephaniah*, New American Commentary (Nashville: Broadman & Holman, 1998), p.58.

25. See, e.g., G. M. Burge, 'Lachish', *NIDOTTE*, vol. 4, pp.862-4; and Alfred J. Hoerth, *Archaeology and the Old Testament* (Grand Rapids: Baker, 1998), pp.347-51.

26. Waltke equates it with Judah ('Micah', p.630).

27. I have translated the verb *nātan* + preposition *'al* as **'give ... to'**; this is perfectly defensible; see *DCH*, vol. 5, p.799.

28. Cf. Andersen and Freedman, *Micah*, pp.234-5.

29. One can't help but love Andersen and Freedman's candour about the latter part of verse 15: 'Nothing could be clearer than v. 15b. The words are familiar and the grammar is flawless. Yet we don't know what Micah is talking about' (*Micah*, p. 236).

30. See L. J. Coppes, *TWOT*, vol. 2, p.815.

31. G. S. Cansdale, *All the Animals of the Bible Lands* (Grand Rapids: Zondervan, 1970), p.142.

32. This is a good reason for assuming that 1:10-16 is original with Micah and not something later editors have tampered with. No subsequent editor would leave a text in such nasty shape, but

would have been sure to smooth it out and clean it up. See Andersen and Freedman, *Micah*, p.246: 'In other words, no scribe would knowingly rewrite a text into the form we now have.'

33. Andersen and Freedman, *Micah*, p.248.

34. *NIDOTTE*, vol. 1, pp.844-5.

35. Compare the procedure in some Muslim countries: instead of charging Christians with a religious crime, authorities will plant 'evidence' and then convict the Christian on drug charges.

36. Bruce Waltke, *A Commentary on Micah* (Grand Rapids: Eerdmans, 2007), p.106.

37. *Ibid.*, p.100.

38. Gary V. Smith captures Micah's dig nicely: 'Isn't it too bad! It is so unfortunate what these rich people had to go through. What they coveted and stole is now being coveted and taken from them. They're going to end up with nothing. Doesn't it just break your heart to see them get what they deserve!' (*Hosea, Amos, Micah*, The NIV Application Commentary, Grand Rapids: Zondervan, 2001, p.465).

39. The **'you'** in verse 5 is singular.

40. Smith comments: 'Hidden behind this devastating word of judgement is also the hopeful implication that some day the faithful people of God will again inherit the land (see Mic. 2:12-13; 7:11-12); the promise to Abraham will be fulfilled in spite of the destruction God will bring on the nation in the near future' (*Hosea, Amos, Micah*, p.466).

41. John Guy, *Queen of Scots* (Boston: Houghton Mifflin, 2004), p.8.

42. See the helpful discussion of *ḥāmad* in Andersen and Freedman, *Micah*, pp.270-72.

43. The verb is *nātap*, used eighteen times in the Old Testament. It can refer to the sky 'pouring down' rain (Judg. 5:4; Ps. 68:8), or to something 'dripping' from lips or hands (S. of S. 4:11; 5:5; see also Joel 3:18; Amos 9:13); then in some contexts it means 'to prophesy' or 'preach' (Ezek. 20:46; 21:2; Amos 7:16). This last is its meaning in our passage. Some think there may be a sarcastic twist to it that picks up the 'dripping' note (i.e., 'Don't drivel...'), but I doubt it. See Shalom M. Paul, *Amos*, Hermeneia (Minneapolis: Fortress, 1991), p.250. Micah uses a form of *nātap* three times in verse 6 and twice in verse 11.

44. Waltke cites Deuteronomy 32:35; 1 Kings 11:3; Isaiah 8:8 (*A Commentary on Micah*, p.113). See also *G-K*, 45o.

45. S. Goldman, 'Micah', *The Twelve Prophets*, Soncino Books of the Bible (London: Soncino, 1985), p.163.

46. Waltke rightly makes this point (*A Commentary on Micah*, p.118). The **'women'** are plural in the first line of verse 9; then Micah seems to picture them individually driven out from, literally, 'the house of her delights / luxuries'.

47. Smith, *Hosea, Amos, Micah*, p.469.

48. Waltke, *A Commentary on Micah*, pp.120, 129.

49. Cf. *BDB*, p.379.

50. See Theodore Laetsch, *The Minor Prophets* (St. Louis: Concordia, 1956), p.255.

51. Helmut Thielicke, *Notes from a Wayfarer* (New York: Paragon House, 1995), p.119.

52. See the 1981 Baker reprint edition of *Calvin's Commentaries*, vol. 14, part 2, pp.211-13.

53. Smith, *Hosea, Amos, Micah*, p.481; see also Andersen and Freedman, *Micah*, p.342.

54. Keil, *The Twelve Minor Prophets,* vol. 1, p.447.

55. *Ibid.*

56. Cf. *NIDOTTE*, vol. 1, pp.1018-19.

57. Cf. Dale Ralph Davis, *2 Samuel: Out of Every Adversity* (Fearn, Ross-shire: Christian Focus, 1999), p.59.

58. Walter C. Kaiser, Jr., *Micah – Malachi*, Communicator's Commentary (Dallas: Word, 1992), p.45.

59. Elizabeth Achtemeier helpfully draws attention to Mark 14:28 and 16:7, where the risen Jesus will 'go before' his disciples to Galilee (*Minor Prophets I,* New International Biblical Commentary, Peabody, MA: Hendrickson, 1996, p.316).

60. Allen, *The Books of Joel ... and Micah,* pp.302-3; Waltke, *A Commentary on Micah,* pp.140-42; Andrew E. Hill and John H. Walton, *A Survey of the Old Testament* (Grand Rapids: Zondervan, 2nd edition, 2000), p.506.

61. Wolff, *Micah,* p.85.

62. Keil, *The Twelve Minor Prophets,* vol. 1, pp.448-9. For more argumentation see, McComiskey, 'Micah', p.415.

63. Cited by Keil, *The Twelve Minor Prophets,* vol. 1, p.448.

64. John Watson, *The Scot of the Eighteenth Century* (New York: A. C. Armstrong, no date), p.194.

2. Through judgement to peace (3:1 – 5:15)

1. Waltke, *A Commentary on Micah,* p.153.

2. See Barker and Bailey, *Micah ... Zephaniah,* pp.74-5; see also Elizabeth Achtemeier, who says:

... *mišpāṭ* was God's order for the covenant community as set forth in the traditions handed down from generation to generation. It was to reflect God's character and commands and was principally designed to restore to their proper place in the community those who had been wronged. Such 'justice' was intended to rescue the endangered, and help the hurt, and secure surcease for those suffering violence. Its aim was not only to punish the wrongdoer but to give aid to the innocent. In short, *mišpāṭ* had a 'saving' function, as can be seen in sentences such as, 'Judge the fatherless' (Isa. 1:17, Hb.), or 'He judged the cause of the poor and needy' (Jer. 22:16, RSV) (*Minor Prophets I*, pp.317-18).

3. Sometimes, sadly and ironically, Micah's rhetoric borders on the literal. One thinks of Heinrich Himmler's 'toys' in his attic: tables and chairs made from parts of human bodies; the seat of one chair was a human pelvis; the legs were human legs on human feet. Then there was a copy of Hitler's *Mein Kampf* with a cover made from human skin taken from someone's back — see Anthony Read, *The Devil's Disciples: Hitler's Inner Circle* (New York: W. W. Norton, 2003), p.851.

4. See Dale Ralph Davis, *Judges: Such a Great Salvation* (Fearn, Ross-shire: Christian Focus, 2000), pp.49-50.

5. Allen, *The Books of Joel ... and Micah,* pp.308-9.

6. Calvin, *Sermons on ... Micah,* p.145 (emphasis mine).

7. See Waltke, *A Commentary on Micah,* p.151; and Keil, *The Twelve Minor Prophets,* vol. 1, pp.450-51.

8. See Wolff, *Micah,* pp.102-3, and Waltke, *A Commentary on Micah,* pp.160-61, for details.

9. Achtemeier, *Minor Prophets I,* p.319. She adds: 'They were perhaps the forerunners of every preacher who would not think of upsetting the largest contributor to the church budget, or of every institution that has named a building after a wealthy scoundrel, or of every university that has given an honorary doctor's degree to an ignorant but generous millionaire' (*Ibid.,* p. 320).

10. On divination, see the article by J. Stafford Wright, *NBD,* 3rd edition, pp.279-80.

11. See Waltke, *A Commentary on Micah,* p.166; Andersen and Freedman, *Micah,* p.377.

12. Wolff, *Micah,* p.105; see also *TLOT,* vol. 2, p.611. Cf. Calvin's comment:

Thus, when Micah proclaims: *But I, I am filled with power from the Spirit of God,* let us realize that Micah is confessing that in himself he is only a man, that he is not boasting of having a keener mind than others in order to glean their praise; rather, he only wants them to recognize what God has put in his soul. Consequently, if we want our Lord to fortify us with power, then let us acknowledge the absence of such in ourselves, and how empty we are of any good. Above all, let those who are charged with preaching the Word of God acknowledge their insufficiency (*Sermons on ... Micah,* p.165).

13. John L. Mackay, *Jonah, Micah, Nahum, Habakkuk, Zephaniah* (Fearn, Ross-shire: Christian Focus, 1998), pp.88-9.
14. C. von Orelli, *The Twelve Minor Prophets* (Minneapolis: Klock and Klock, 1977 [first published 1897]), p.201.
15. The verb form is best taken as an infinitive absolute, as Waltke argues (*A Commentary on Micah,* p.178).
16. See *BDB,* pp.196-7; *NIDOTTE,* vol. 1, pp.963-4.
17. See Carl G. Rasmussen, *Zondervan NIV Atlas of the Bible* (Grand Rapids: Zondervan, 1989), p.135; Mackay, *Jonah ... Zephaniah,* p.89; and John Bright, *A History of Israel,* 3rd edition (Philadelphia: Westminster, 1981), p.284.
18. C. F. Keil points to King Jehoiakim's way of oppressing labourers at a later period of history (Jer. 22:13-17) and King Ahab's earlier 'removal' of a recalcitrant Naboth (1 Kings 21).
19. Micah mentions that the priests **'teach'**. This was one of their primary duties (cf. Deut. 33:8-11; Mal. 2:4-7). Sometimes one wonders if contemporary churches don't take their cues from Judah's leadership. In some churches one almost wants to skip public worship for the whole month of November while the church harps on about money and giving to meet the next year's budget, inserting 'commercials' about giving and 'plugs' for the budget into worship services and beating the money drum for all it's worth.
20. Allen, *The Books of Joel ... and Micah,* p.318.
21. Cited by V. P. Hamilton in *TWOT,* vol. 2, p.914.
22. On the importance of this text, see Dale Ralph Davis, *1 Kings: The Wisdom and the Folly* (Fearn, Ross-shire: Christian Focus, 2002/2007), pp.65-7.
23. Calvin hits the mark:

So long, therefore, as hypocrites trust in God's promises, without thinking too much about God, they imagine God to be on their side and in approval of their conduct. In brief, they want to keep God in their pocket, and treat him like a little child, who, when he becomes upset, can be mollified with a toy and forced to condescend to their will. That is how hypocrites treat God's promises, while mocking him and his majesty in total disregard of his Word (*Sermons on ... Micah,* pp.181-2).

24. McComiskey, 'Micah', p.420; see also A. F. Rainey, 'Zion', *ISBE,* vol. 4, pp.1198-9.

25. J. H. Walton, V. H. Matthews and M. W. Chavalas, *The IVP Bible Background Commentary: Old Testament* (Downers Grove, IL: InterVarsity, 2000), p.783.

26. See Andersen and Freedman, *Micah,* p.385; and John L. Mackay, *Jeremiah* (Fearn, Ross-shire: Christian Focus, 2004, 2 vols), vol. 2, p.128.

27. David Prior helpfully connects 3:12 with 1 Kings 9:1-9 (*The Message of Joel, Micah & Habakkuk,* The Bible Speaks Today, Leicester: Inter-Varsity, 1998, p.145).

28. Walter Kaiser levels a searing application along these lines (*Micah – Malachi,* p.52).

29. See James L. Mays, *Micah,* Old Testament Library (Philadelphia: Westminster, 1976), p.95; and Wolff, *Micah,* pp.114, 116-18.

30. Style-conscious translations omit the **'and'**; I found that only NASB retains it this way, and AV and NJB recognize it as an adversative ('but'); NKJV uses 'now'.

31. The phrase (Heb., *'aḥărît hayyāmîm*) occurs fourteen times in the Old Testament (Gen. 49:1; Num. 24:14; Deut. 4:30; 31:29; Isa. 2:2 = Micah 4:1; Jer. 23:20; 30:24; 48:47; 49:39; Ezek. 38:16; Dan. 2:28; 10:14; Hosea 3:5). See for discussion, Andersen and Freedman, *Micah,* pp.401-2; McComiskey, 'Micah', pp.421-2; and R. L. Harris, *TWOT,* vol. 1, p.34.

32. On temple mountains in ancient Near-Eastern religion, see Othmar Keel, *The Symbolism of the Biblical World* (New York: Crossroad, 1985), pp.113-20; and Waltke, *A Commentary on Micah,* p.195.

33. Alec Motyer, *Isaiah,* Tyndale Old Testament Commentaries (Leicester: Inter-Varsity, 1999), p.51. Ortlund speaks of the 'anti-gravitational anomaly of this human river flowing uphill to worship God' (Raymond C. Ortlund, Jr., *Isaiah: God Saves Sinners,* Preaching the Word, Wheaton: Crossway, 2005, p.51).

34. 'It is not as tourists going sightseeing that the nations will come to Jerusalem. They are there as disciples who want to take

full advantage of the teaching available in the temple' (Mackay, *Jonah ... Zephaniah*, p.94).

35. Arthur Fawcett, *The Cambuslang Revival* (London: Banner of Truth Trust, 1971), p.211.

36. Keil, *The Twelve Minor Prophets*, vol. 1, pp.460-61; and Smith, *Hosea, Amos, Micah*, pp.512-13.

37. See 1 Samuel 13:20-21, and R. F. Youngblood, '1, 2 Samuel,' *Expositor's Bible Commentary* (Grand Rapids: Zondervan, 1992, 12 vols), vol. 3, pp.59-60; and, generally, J. I. Packer, M. C. Tenney, and W. White, *The Bible Almanac* (Nashville: Thomas Nelson, 1980), pp.268, 274-6.

38. Micah's picture here shows 'converted' nations (4:2-3); this does not negate, for example, Joel's description of the rebellious nations meeting judgement (Joel 3:9-17).

39. Waltke, *A Commentary on Micah*, p.200.

40. Walton, Matthews and Chavalas, *The IVP Bible Background Commentary: Old Testament*, p.783.

41. See M. Van Pelt and W. C. Kaiser, Jr., *NIDOTTE*, vol. 2, p.264 (on *ḥārad*).

42. Cf. *NIDOTTE*, vol. 4, pp.1297-8.

43. See Keil, *The Twelve Minor Prophets*, vol. 1, p.458.

44. Contrary to the view of Waltke, who prefers a concessive sense ('although') — see *A Commentary on Micah*, pp.202-3.

45. Smith, *Hosea, Amos, Micah*, pp.509-10. A perennial question comes up with Micah 4:1-4 and Isaiah 2:1-4: which is 'original', or do they both draw on some common prophetic teaching? I don't know. You can read the commentaries and discover that others don't know. Note, however, that contextually Isaiah 2:1-4 functions in the same way as Micah 4:1-4: after the overwhelmingly negative tone of Isaiah 1, Isaiah 2:1-4 still insists that there is a 'stubborn future' which Judah's sin cannot erase from Yahweh's calendar.

46. Cited in Colin and Mary Peckham, *Sounds from Heaven* (Fearn, Ross-shire: Christian Focus, 2004), pp.125-6.

47. Thielicke, *Notes from a Wayfarer*, pp.165-6.

48. Calvin captures the tone of the passage well:

> The meaning briefly is, that though the Church differed nothing for a time from a dead man, or at least from one that is maimed, no despair ought to be entertained; for the Lord sometimes raises up his people, as though he raised the dead from the grave: and this fact ought to be carefully noticed, for as soon as the Church of God does not shine

forth, we think that it is wholly extinct and destroyed. But
the Church is so preserved in the world, that it sometimes
rises again from death: in short, the preservation of the
Church, almost every day, is accompanied with many mir-
acles (*Calvin's Commentaries,* vol. 14, part 2, p. 275).

49. *BDB*, p.229.
50. See Mackay, *Jonah ... Zephaniah,* p.96, and McComiskey,
'Micah', p.423. McComiskey says, 'To Micah the remnant was
more than simply a residue of people. It was the repository of
God's grace and promise as well as the force that would ultimately
conquer the godless nations at the end time (5:8-15). It is thus an
act of grace that forms these poor exiles into a remnant and
bestows on them the blessings of the Messianic Age (cf. Rom.
11:1-6).'
51. Calvin, *Sermons on the Book of Micah,* p.232.
52. Waltke, *A Commentary on Micah,* p.231.
53. *ABD*, vol. 5, p.26.
54. I take the conjunction in an explicative or emphatic sense
(hence the translation **'yes'**); cf. R. J. Williams, *Hebrew Syntax: An
Outline* (Toronto: University of Toronto, 2nd edition, 1976), p.71;
B. K. Waltke and M. O'Connor, *An Introduction to Biblical Hebrew
Syntax* (Winona Lake, IN: Eisenbrauns, 1990), pp.652-3.
55. You won't see this structure in the NIV. For some reason it
omits the 'now' in 5:1 and does not allow it to stand out in 4:9. The
NASB, ESV, or NRSV are better guides here.
56. See Mackay, *Jonah ... Zephaniah,* pp.98-9.
57. See Longman in *NIDOTTE*, vol. 3, pp.1082-3. The cognate
noun follows the verb here — literally, 'to shout a shouting'.
58. See Barker's very helpful summary of the matter in Barker and
Bailey, *Micah ... Zephaniah,* pp.90-91.
59. Cf. *K-B*, vol. 1, p.189.
60. This is the only occurrence of *gā'al* (to redeem) in Micah. Alec
Motyer nicely summarizes its use and significance when he says
that:

[The term] stresses the person of the redeemer, his relationship to the redeemed and his intervention on their
behalf. The participle *gō'ēl* is the technical term for the next-
of-kin who has the right to take his helpless relative's needs
as his own (Lv. 25:25; Nu. 5:8), and is often used of the
'avenger' of a murdered person. This is a good indication of
the substitutionary nature of the relationship (the one being

dead, the other taking over and acting; Nu. 35:12; Dt. 19:6).
In its classical expression the work of 'redeemer' was a right
which no other dare usurp (Ru. 3:12; 4:1-6). It was a right
rather than an inescapable duty, calling for willingness. It
speaks here [Isa. 35:9], therefore, of the Lord as the only
one who can redeem his people, identifying with them as
their next-of-kin, willingly shouldering, on their helpless
behalf and in their place, all and every one of their needs,
paying their price (Lv. 27:13,19,31) (*The Prophecy of Isaiah*,
Downers Grove, IL: Inter-Varsity, 1993, p.275).

61. Barker and Bailey, *Micah ... Zephaniah*, p.91.
62. Cf. Leslie, *IDB*, vol. 3, p.371; B. W. Anderson, *Understanding
the Old Testament* (Englewood Cliffs, NJ: Prentice-Hall, 4th edition,
1986), p.337.
63. Peckham, *Sounds from Heaven*, p.183.
64. Achtemeier, *Minor Prophets I*, p.335.
65. Keil, *The Twelve Minor Prophets*, vol. 1, p.474. Others view the
'many nations' as a reference to the various mercenaries compris-
ing Sennacherib's army in 701 BC (cf. Bruce Waltke and Gary
Smith). However, 'many nations' probably 'does not refer to either
the Babylonians or Assyrians, for, while there were different
national groups in each of those imperial armies, they did not form
several nations' (Kaiser, *Micah – Malachi*, p.62); see also Andersen
and Freedman, *Micah*, pp.455-7.
66. For some of the imagery Hillers draws attention to Isaiah
41:15-16 and Jeremiah 51:33 (*Micah*, Hermeneia, Philadelphia:
Fortress, 1984, p.61).
67. On the horns, cf. J. J. Niehaus, *God at Sinai* (Grand Rapids:
Zondervan, 1995), pp.226-7 (note); and Goldman, 'Micah', p.173.
68. Jackie A. Naude, in *NIDOTTE*, vol. 2, p.277.
69. William L. Shirer, *The Nightmare Years: 1930–1940* (Boston:
Little, Brown, 1984), p.618.
70. See *Westminster Shorter Catechism*, number 26.
71. Cf. *NIDOTTE*, vol. 1, pp.819-21.
72. Waltke, *A Commentary on Micah*, p.263.
73. In my view Waltke (*A Commentary on Micah*, p.298) has to
imagine too much to make this fit Sennacherib and his army. On
the 'Babylon' view, see Achtemeier, *Minor Prophets I*, p.338; and
Wolff, *Micah*, pp.142-3.
74. Keil, *The Twelve Minor Prophets*, vol. 1, p.483.
75. Laetsch, *The Minor Prophets*, p.271.
76. Cf. *BDB*, p.605; Keil, *The Twelve Minor Prophets*, vol. 1, p.479.

77. See especially B. B. Warfield's article, 'The Divine Messiah in the Old Testament,' *Biblical and Theological Studies* (Philadelphia: Presbyterian and Reformed, 1952), pp.79-126.

78. Cf. discussion in Waltke, *A Commentary on Micah,* pp.276-7 (the reference cited on p.277 as Isa. 61:9,11 is a misprint; it should be Isa. 63:9,11).

79. Matthew includes the chief priests and scribes' citing of Micah 5:2 in his account of the arrival of the Magi. They wanted to find 'the king of the Jews' (Matt. 2:2), and this troubled Herod, which in turn troubled Jerusalem, because when Herod was troubled it meant trouble (Matt. 2:3). He assembles the professors of systematic theology and Old Testament to find out where the Messiah was to be born (Matt. 2:4), and they answer, 'Bethlehem', citing Micah 5:2. One might wonder why Matthew included this in his Gospel. Perhaps he had an apologetic purpose. One of the standing Jewish objections to Jesus' messiahship was that he was from Galilee, not Bethlehem (John 7:41-42,52). Perhaps those who pressed home this seemingly obvious point would say, 'Read your Bible, man!' Matthew may be answering this position, as if to say, 'He may be from Nazareth and Galilee, but Jesus was *born* in Bethlehem, as the prophet said; check the courthouse records, man!'

80. Calvin, *Sermons on the Book of Micah,* p.277.

81. In *Lange's Commentary* (see note 96 below for details).

82. See discussion in Barker and Bailey, *Micah ... Zephaniah,* p.99.

83. See Keil, *The Twelve Minor Prophets,* vol. 1, pp.483-4.

84. *Ibid.,* pp.484-5; cf. also Williams, *Hebrew Syntax,* p.52 (no. 293).

85. See Allen, *The Books of Joel ... and Micah,* pp.345 6. Allen identifies the **'rest of his brothers'** with northern Israelites, but the stress on future unity remains.

86. See Keil, *The Twelve Minor Prophets,* vol. 1, pp.484-5; Waltke, *A Commentary on Micah,* pp.281, 302. Some would see this fulfilled in the conversion of thousands of Israelites after Pentecost (cf. Acts 2:41,47; so *New Geneva Study Bible*); others might look beyond that to what Romans 11:23-27 describes (obviously, this depends on how one understands 'all Israel' in verse 26).

87. Calvin, *Sermons on the Book of Micah,* p.281.

88. E. B. Pusey, *The Minor Prophets: A Commentary,* 2 vols. (Grand Rapids: Baker, 1968 reprint), vol. 2, p.73.

89. Cormac O'Brien, *Secret Lives of the U. S. Presidents* (Philadelphia: Quirk Books, 2004), p.48.

90. **'Assyria'** occurs here as an enemy apparently faced during Messiah's reign (5:4) and hence also after the time when Yahweh 'gives up' his people to dominance by others (5:3); Micah uses the name of the eighth-century BC enemy for any enemy that might threaten during Messiah's regime. On this, cf. McComiskey, 'Micah', p. 429, and Achtemeier, *Minor Prophets I*, p.342. Note also how the prophets will use, for example, Edom in a typical sense (Isa. 34:5-6; Ezek. 35); cf. Ortlund, *Isaiah: God Saves Sinners*, p.196; and H. L. Ellison, *Ezekiel: The Man and His Message* (Grand Rapids: Eerdmans, 1956), pp.122-4.

91. On the numerical aspect, see Gary V. Smith, *Amos* (Fearn, Ross-shire: Christian Focus, 1998), pp.69-70.

92. The second line of verse 6 says they will shepherd **'the land of Nimrod at** [or, 'in'] **its entrances'**. However, NIV and NRSV follow an alternative reading. If two letters in **'entrances'** are reversed the word becomes 'drawn sword'. This forms a good parallel with the 'sword' in the preceding line. There is some evidence in the versions for this. For discussion, see Waltke, *A Commentary on Micah*, p.292. I have retained the reading of the traditional Hebrew text.

93. Mark D. Futato, *NIDOTTE*, vol. 2, p.363.

94. *Ibid.*, vol. 3, p.1041.

95. I cannot agree with Achtemeier, who thinks the stress is on the mysterious character of the dew rather than its beneficial effect (*Minor Prophets I*, p.344). **'Showers'** don't seem so mysterious and they are part of the comparison too.

96. Paul Kleinert, 'The Book of Micah,' in *Lange's Commentary on the Holy Scriptures*, vol. 7, *Ezekiel – Malachi* (Grand Rapids: Zondervan, 1960 [first published 1868]), p.37.

97. Andersen and Freedman, *Micah*, p.486.

98. See Hillers, *Micah*, p.70; and Barker and Bailey, *Micah ... Zephaniah*, p.104. For the request/address-to-God view, see Waltke, *A Commentary on Micah*, p.313.

99. See, e.g., Hillers, *Micah*, p.71.

100. I think Yahweh is addressing Israel or the 'remnant of Jacob' in these verses. Achtemeier argues (partly picking up on verse 15) that the Gentiles are in view (*Minor Prophets I*, pp.346-7). But Isaiah, Micah's contemporary, charges Judah with these very sins (Isa. 2:6-11). And verse 15 (vengeance on disobedient nations) simply reaffirms what Micah had stated in verse 9.

101. See Waltke, *A Commentary on Micah*, p.336.

102. Achtemeier, *Minor Prophets I*, p.347.

103. See Nahum M. Sarna, *Understanding Genesis* (New York: Schocken, 1970), pp.11-12.

104. See J. A. Motyer, 'Idolatry', *NBD*, 3rd edition, p.496; on the conception and care of images in the Ancient Near East, see *ABD*, vol. 3, pp.376-9.

105. Many want to emend **'cities'** at the end of verse 14, in an attempt to find something more appropriately parallel to 'Asherah poles' in the first line of the verse. However, the text is solid and alternative proposals don't get beyond guesswork. See especially Barker and Bailey, *Micah ... Zephaniah*, p.106; for all the details, see Waltke, *A Commentary on Micah*, pp.327-8.

106. Calvin, *Sermons from the Book of Micah*, p.297.

107. See the fine article by H. G. L. Peels, *NIDOTTE*, vol. 3, pp.154-6.

108. See Arnold Dallimore, *Spurgeon* (Chicago: Moody, 1984), p.130.

109. See Barbara W. Tuchman, *The March of Folly* (New York: Alfred A. Knopf, 1984), pp.19-23.

3. Through judgement to pardon (6:1 – 7:20)

1. Mackay, *Jonah ... Zephaniah*, p.115; Allen, *The Books of Joel ... and Micah*, p.364.

2. Waltke, *A Commentary on Micah*, p.344. For discussion on *rîb*, see G. Liedke, *TLOT*, vol. 3, pp.1232-7.

3. Late Bronze Age treaties would list large numbers of gods and goddesses as witnesses, as well as deified elements of the natural world, but monotheism 'de-deifies' the world, and so witnesses in Scripture are very much non-divine heavens and earth (Deut. 32:1; Isa. 1:2), or mountains (here), or memorial stones (Josh. 24:27). Cf. *ABD*, vol. 1, p.1181; K. A. Kitchen, *Ancient Orient and Old Testament* (Chicago: Inter-Varsity, 1966), p.97.

4. Waltke, *A Commentary on Micah*, pp.348-9.

5. Cf. *TDOT*, vol. 7, pp.395-6; *NIDOTTE*, vol. 2, pp.748-9.

6. On **'ransomed'** (*pādâ*), see W. B. Coker, *TWOT*, vol. 2, pp.716-17.

7. Allen, *The Books of Joel ... and Micah*, p.366; see also Mackay, *Jonah ... Zephaniah*, p.117.

8. See, e.g., Hosea 5:8; Ps. 18:41 (18:42 in Hebrew); Eccles. 5:10 (5:9 in Hebrew).

9. See Allen, *The Books of Joel ... and Micah*, p.369. On 'righteousness', note especially M. A. Seifrid, 'Righteousness, Justice, and Justification', *New Dictionary of Biblical Theology* (Leicester:

Inter-Varsity, 2000), pp.740-45; H. G. Stigers, *TWOT*, vol. 2, pp.752-5; and Motyer, *The Prophecy of Isaiah*, p.405.
10. See *NIDOTTE*, vol. 1, pp.1100-1103 (L. C. Allen on *zākar*).
11. See Waltke, *A Commentary on Micah*, pp.378, 385.
12. See Mackay, *Jonah ... Zephaniah*, p.118; Allen, *The Books of Joel ... and Micah*, p.370.
13. *NBD*, p.844.
14. See the discussions in Andersen and Freedman, *Micah*, pp.532-8. Note that such sacrifice consisted of human offspring — not necessarily restricted to infants. See further, John E. Hartley, *Leviticus*, Word Biblical Commentary (Dallas: Word, 1992), pp.334-7.
15. McComiskey, 'Micah', p.436.
16. Smith, *Hosea, Amos, Micah*, p.553.
17. Mackay, *Jonah ... Zephaniah*, p.120. Andersen and Freedman point out that the combination to 'love *ḥesed*' occurs only here in the Hebrew Bible; to 'do' *ḥesed* is a more usual expression (*Micah*, p. 528). Gary Smith claims that Micah's 'loving *ḥesed*' probably goes far beyond glad delight in treating others justly and mercifully; it may well point to the whole, across-the-board response that an Israelite is to have towards Yahweh's *ḥesed*. He writes:

> On a day when one is not required to be merciful to any unfortunate person, one is still involved with maintaining a faithful covenant relationship with God and other people within the covenant. In other words, loving to maintain steadfast covenant loyalty will impact a person's attitude to worshipping God on the Sabbath, leaving the land fallow every seven years, releasing slaves according to Mosaic instructions, caring for the poor, and giving a tithe each year. If there is no commitment to remain faithful to this divine covenant relationship, then covenant life will cease to exist. Understood in this way, *ḥsd* is a broad term that encompasses much more than merely acting mercifully toward others (*Hosea, Amos, Micah*, p.554).

Because of this I wonder if there is an almost humorous undertow to the 'simple' formula, **'What does God require ... except...?'** If Gary Smith is right, Micah's formula is similar to that of Moses in Deuteronomy 10:12-13, where the demand is intensely serious but the form almost comical — i.e., 'What does Yahweh require of you except a whole-souled, mind-dominating, love-directed, life-consuming devotion, showing itself in total and complete obedience?' That's all he asks — really! What could be simpler than that?!

18. See, e.g., *TDOT,* vol. 12, pp.420-21.

19. Walking **'carefully'** can well embrace 'walking discerningly' (see Waltke, *A Commentary on Micah,* p.394); this latter could indicate that one rightly sees and feels the claim implicit in Yahweh's acts of grace (6:3-5) and responds appropriately.

20. *BDB,* p. 641.

21. See Waltke, *A Commentary on Micah,* p.397. Waltke prefers to see *nś'*, 'to forgive', here.

22. For other possible rip-offs, see Hillers, *Micah,* p.82. John Mackay points out that some would have paid their rents in kind and mean-minded landlords could have cheated them on those occasions (*Jonah ... Zephaniah,* p.123). On the weights and measures, see *NBD,* pp.1236-7.

23. Waltke and O'Connor, *An Introduction to Biblical Hebrew Syntax,* pp.489-90 (30.5.1e).

24. I do not take the **'you'** as necessarily referring to the nation's ruler (as Waltke does), but to any representative guilty Judean.

25. See Andersen and Freedman, *Micah,* p.549.

26. Waltke, *A Commentary on Micah,* p.403.

27. Keil, *The Twelve Minor Prophets,* vol. 1, p.501.

28. *Ibid.,* p.502.

29. Calvin, *Sermons on the Book of Micah,* p.344.

30. Marvin Olasky, *The American Leadership Tradition* (Wheaton, IL: Crossway, 2000), p.127.

31. A. M. Renwick, *The Story of the Scottish Reformation* (Grand Rapids: Eerdmans, 1960), p.148.

32. Andersen and Freedman, *Micah,* p.567.

33. See R. K. Harrison, 'Fig', *ISBE,* vol. 2, pp.301-2.

34. See Mackay, *Jonah ... Zephaniah,* p.126.

35. See *New Bible Commentary,* 4th edition, p. 490 (on Ps. 4).

36. Cf. Ronald Reagan's proposal for the nine most terrifying words in the English language: 'I'm from the government, and I'm here to help' (Cited by Thomas E. Woods, Jr., *The Politically Incorrect Guide to American History,* Washington: Regnery, 2004, p.232).

37. See Keil, *The Twelve Minor Prophets,* vol. 1, p.504.

38. Waltke, *A Commentary on Micah,* p.426.

39. See McComiskey, 'Micah', p.441.

40. The verb for **'weave ... together'** (*'ābat*) is used only here, but it has cognates that make its meaning reasonably certain (see *BDB,* p.721).

41. My reading, **'the most upright a thorn hedge'**, follows a proposal to redivide the consonantal text so that the first '*m*' in *mimmĕsûkâ* becomes the suffix on *yāšār* (**'upright'**).

42. **'Panic time'** is *mĕbûkâ*, on which see Motyer, *The Prophecy of Isaiah*, p.183. There (Isa. 22:5) it refers to the terror and confusion in the wake of an attack.

43. I suppose one could see this breakdown in relationships as occurring under the conditions of the coming punishment (7:4b), but I think Micah probably intends to describe the current conditions in Judah as in verses 2-4a.

44. Cf. J. Kühlewein, in *TLOT*, vol. 3, pp.1243-4; and E. H. Merrill, in *NIDOTTE*, vol. 1, pp.415-16.

45. Allen, *The Books of Joel ... and Micah*, p.388.

46. These examples come from an article by Marvin Olasky and from field reports of Voice of the Martyrs.

47. For brief orientation on *sph* and *yhl*, see *NIDOTTE*, vol. 3, pp.831-2; vol. 2, pp.435-6.

48. Mackay, *Jonah ... Zephaniah*, p.129.

49, Allen, *The Books of Joel ... and Micah*, p.393.

50. Allen prefers the early post-exilic period (pp. 251, 393). Waltke sees the initial historical situation as the Assyrian crisis under Hezekiah (*A Commentary on Micah*, pp.433, 451), while Gary Smith settles for some time after Hezekiah, in Manasseh's reign, with a view to Babylon's conquest (*Hosea, Amos, Micah*, p.573).

51. Mackay, *Jonah ... Zephaniah*, p.131.

52. See McComiskey, 'Micah', p.443.

53. Keil, *The Twelve Minor Prophets*, vol. 1, pp.508-9; and Waltke, *A Commentary on Micah*, p.435.

54. Waltke, *A Commentary on Micah*, p.452.

55. See Allen, *The Books of Joel ... and Micah*, p.395.

56. So Waltke, *A Commentary on Micah*, p.435; and Kleinert (in *Lange's Commentary*). Both imperfect verb forms are prefixed with a 'simple *waw*', and these frequently seem to have a non-indicative sense.

57. Mackay, *Jonah ... Zephaniah*, p.130.

58. See Andersen and Freedman, *Micah*, p.584.

59. Waltke thinks **'righteousness'** (also feminine) is the antecedent here rather than **'enemy'** (*A Commentary on Micah*, p.436).

60. *Calvin's Commentaries*, vol. 14, part 2, p.373.

61. See Mackay, *Jonah ... Zephaniah*, pp.132-3, and McComiskey, 'Micah', p.443, for discussion of where we should place the primary fulfilment of this piece.

62. Even in Ezra 9:9 it does not refer to a city wall — it is metaphorical of Yahweh's protection (see ESV and even NIV). Anyway, the repaired ruins in that verse were the walls of the temple, not those of the city. See Waltke, *A Commentary on Micah,* p.456; Smith, *Hosea, Amos, Micah,* p.574.

63. Cf. *BDB,* p.349.

64. Keil, *The Twelve Minor Prophets,* vol. 1, p.510. See also Smith, *Hosea, Amos, Micah,* p.575.

65. Micah seems to use here not the normal, but a poetic name for Egypt, *māṣôr,* possibly meaning 'Affliction place'; see its use in Isa. 19:6; 37:25; cf. Waltke, *A Commentary on Micah,* p.456.

66. Keil, *The Twelve Minor Prophets,* vol. 1, p.511.

67. Some doctor verse 15 (see NRSV, NJB, REB, TEV), so that all of verses 14-17 are Micah's prayer without an 'interruption' from Yahweh. One has to admire such commitment to consistency, but each of these versions recognizes that it is 'correcting' the text.

68. If Micah had clearly wanted to express assertion and prediction, he could have used a perfect form of the verb with a prefixed *waw*-conjunctive, as in 5:4-6 (5:3-5 in Hebrew). See Andersen and Freedman, *Micah,* p.591, for discussion.

69. Mays, *Micah,* p.164; Smith, *Hosea, Amos, Micah,* p.576.

70. In 3:12 *ya'ar* is used when the temple mount is destined to become an 'overgrown' height.

71. See the articles by I. Cornelius in *NIDOTTE,* vol. 2, pp.492-4, 725.

72. Keil, *The Twelve Minor Prophets,* vol. 1, p.512.

73. It almost seems as though Micah's allusion to **'as in days of long ago'** at the end of verse 14 triggers Yahweh's **'as in the days when you came out from the land of Egypt'** in verse 15.

74. Keil takes verses 16-17 as a continuation of Yahweh's word in verse 15 and so attributes all of 15-17 to Yahweh (*The Twelve Minor Prophets,* vol. 1, p. 513). However, **'to Yahweh our God'** and **'be afraid of you'** (= Yahweh) in verse 17 indicate that the prophet is speaking.

75. Mackay, *Jonah ... Zephaniah,* p.135; see also Calvin, *Calvin's Commentaries,* vol. 14, part 2, p.396.

76. Waltke, *A Commentary on Micah,* p.444.

77. *Ibid.,* p.462.

78. Read Faith Cook's account of how Micah 7:8-9 played a pivotal role in the restoration of Wang Ming-Dao in *Singing in the Fire* (Edinburgh: Banner of Truth, 1995), pp.21-32.

79. O'Brien, *Secret Lives of the U. S. Presidents,* p.62.

80. Cited in George M. Marsden, *Jonathan Edwards: A Life* (New Haven: Yale University, 2003), p.185.

81. See Alex Luc, in *NIDOTTE*, vol. 2, pp.87-8, for a summary; and handily, Motyer, *Look to the Rock*, p.131.

82. One can rightly translate 1 Peter 2:24 in this vein: 'He himself carried our sins in his body up to the tree' (or, 'upon the tree'). In any case, the idea of another carrying our load of guilt is clear.

83. The phrase could be taken as 'the remnant which is his inheritance'; cf. Waltke, *A Commentary on Micah*, p.445.

84. See John Oswalt's brief but fine summary in *TWOT*, vol. 1, p.430.

85. See Keil, *The Twelve Minor Prophets*, vol. 1, p.515; and Andersen and Freedman, *Micah*, p.599.

86. For further discussion on the promise to the patriarchs (what I call the 'quad promise'), see Dale Ralph Davis, *The Word Became Fresh* (Fearn, Ross-shire: Christian Focus, 2006), pp.31-43.

87. 'Rich in *ḥesed* and *'ĕmet'* is 'full of grace and truth' in John 1:14, so that phrase from Exodus 34:6 describes the incarnate Word. Much ink has been spilled on the use of *ḥesed* and, in my view, some of the best of it will be found in F. I. Andersen's essay, 'Yahweh, the Kind and Sensitive God', in *God Who is Rich in Mercy: Essays Presented to D. B. Knox*, ed. P. T. O'Brien and D. G. Peterson (Homebush West, NSW: Lancer Books, 1986), pp.41-88.

88. G. F. Barbour, *The Life of Alexander Whyte, D.D.* (London: Hodder and Stoughton, 1923), pp.316-17.

89. Peggy Noonan, *When Character Was King: A Story of Ronald Reagan* (New York: Viking, 2001), pp.14-15.